YORKSHIRE

Whys . . . Wherefores . . . Whats . . . and Whens

Yorkshire is a kingdom in miniature, with five universities, five cathedrals, mountains, moors, potholes, slag heaps, smoke and fumes and a lot of catarrh. Yorkshiremen are suspicious, obstinate, materialist, isolationist, nonconformist and blunt – and I like them as they are.

Bishop Eric Treacy

YORKSHIRE

Whys . . . Wherefores . . . Whats . . . and Whens

Records and other home truths from England's greatest county

Dalesman Books · 1991

The Dalesman Publishing Company Ltd.
Clapham, Lancaster, LA2 8EB.
(in the "old" county of Yorkshire!)

First published 1987
Reprinted 1987
Second edition 1989
Third edition 1991
Dalesman Publishing Company Ltd. 1987, 1989, 1991
ISBN 1 85568 036 X

*The publishers thank Joshua Tetley & Son Ltd
and Tim Arnold & Associates Ltd
for their assistance in producing this book.*

*Research by Hilary Gray
Illustrations by Roy Ullyett*

Typeset by Lands Services, East Molesey, Surrey KT8 0HY
Printed by Peter Fretwell & Sons Ltd, Keighley, West Yorkshire BD21 1PZ

CONTENTS

INTRODUCTION

Yorkshire as a county changed dramatically with the 1974 administrative reorganisation – changes which served not only to confuse the media and inhabitants, but to bamboozle newcomers and outsiders alike.

The "old" Yorkshire boasted an acreage of 3,923,359 – more acres than there are letters in the Bible! (3,566,840) and it's an area packed with history, personalities and places of interest.

As far as space allows, we've tried to cover as many aspects as possible of life in the "real Yorkshire" (see page 8), excluding areas such as Bowland, Dentdale/ Garsdale and Teesdale which were transferred to other counties in 1974.

If you are keen to conduct your own research into the fascinating whys and wherefores of Yorkshire – or to establish your own records! – we would be delighted to hear from readers who may have items they'd like us to include next time round.

Now read on . . .

To the best of our knowledge, all facts and figures in "Yorkshire Whys . . . Wherefores . . . Whats and Whens" are correct at the time of going to press, but if you beg to differ over any aspect or to give us new information, the address to write to is:
**DALESMAN BOOKS, CLAPHAM,
VIA LANCASTER, LA2 8EB**

The Real Yorkshire

J. Dargan contributed this letter to "The Dalesman"

Quite needless confusion seems to have arisen, over the past few years, as to what is meant by the term "Yorkshire." Yorkshire and its Ridings have existed as a geographical entity for over 1,100 years and it was only in the last century that county councils were set up bearing the name Riding. This was because the area they covered corresponded with the boundaries of the Ridings. It was these councils, not the Ridings, which were abolished in 1974 and replaced with new ones. Parliament has no power to alter or abolish the Ridings as was made clear in a government statement at the time, that "the new names are for local government administration only; for all other reasons Yorkshire is still Yorkshire."

The media, aided by the Post Office, have mainly been responsible for affording the new counties a geographical status denied them by Parliament. This has given rise to an assumption that Yorkshire now consists only of North, South and West Yorks. This is not true. Hull and Middlesbrough are still as much part of Yorkshire as they have ever been, although they are governed by councils not having a Yorkshire title. The Ridings are still legally acceptable terms and can be used freely on legal documentation, including birth certificates.

I hope this clarifies the position for your readers, whichever Riding they live in. We Yorkshire folk must respect our own boundaries if we are to expect the foreign masses to do the same!

EARLY DAYS

First settlers: The first humans arrived in Yorkshire about 10,000 years ago, at the end of the last Ice Age. At that time, Stone Age hunters were able to wander from North Germany without getting their feet wet as Britain was still joined by land to Continental Europe.

First dwelling places: Caves, such as Kirkdale Cave near Pickering and Victoria Cave near Settle.

First Romans: The first Roman occupation was around AD70.

Last tribe of Ancient Britons to be subdued by the Romans: The Brigantes.

First Vikings: Around 800 AD. They settled the boundaries of Yorkshire which we knew until 1974 by dividing it into three Ridings. The word "Riding" came from their "thriding" or third.

GENERAL INFORMATION

Today's Population . . . (figures available are those of the local government areas)

West Yorkshire:	2,067,000
South Yorkshire:	1,295,000
Humberside:	856,000
North Yorkshire:	722,000

There are seven cities – more than any other county, their populations ranging from 712,000 at Leeds to 14,265 at Ripon.

Leeds:	712,000
Sheffield:	527,000
Bradford:	468,000
Wakefield:	314,000
Hull:	247,000
York:	100,600
Ripon:	14,265

Number of Parishes: 1,500

Yorkshire is still the largest geographical county in England and Wales. North Yorkshire County Council governs a larger area than any other County Council in England and Wales.

TOWNS AND CITIES

Richest town in England: Northallerton, on the basis of tax paid per head of population.

Cleanest industrial city in Europe: Sheffield.

Britain's oldest holiday centre: Scarborough.

Largest funfair in Great Britain: Hull fair, held in October. Originally started late 13th century, it has been in Walton Street since 1883.

Oldest city: York (Eboracum), founded AD71.

Largest city: Leeds.

Largest open-air market: Barnsley, with about 370 stallholders and an average letting of over 900 a week. The May Day Green Market was granted a Royal Charter in 1249.

Largest toy fair: Harrogate.

Most complete walled city: York (2½ miles of wall).

Highest market town: Hawes is said to be the highest in England, although there are other claimants.

Longest street name: Land of Green Ginger, Hull.

Narrowest Street: Possibly the Shambles at York where the buildings overhang and it is possible for two people to shake hands across the street from upstairs windows.

Strangest street names: Whip-ma-whop-ma-gate, York's shortest street.
Football, Yeadon, near Leeds.
A lane called "All Alone" in Bradford.

"Firsts"

First hospital (in the country): Opened in York early in the 10th century by the canons of York Minster and dedicated to St. Peter. The hospital was suppressed in 1539 by Henry VIII.

Halifax's first Wild West Show: 1903.

Town Traditions

Scarborough: On Shrove Tuesday, the residents can be seen skipping on the foreshore with skipping ropes stretched across the road! On the same day, the "Pancake Bell" is rung at noon from the Rotunda Museum – after that, you can begin frying pancakes, if you're not too exhausted, that is, by your skipping efforts.

Whitby: The planting of the Penny Hedge, or Horngarth. An annual tradition which is said to date back to 1159 – a ceremonial planting of twigs at Whitby harbour, originally a condition imposed by a murdered hermit before he would grant forgiveness to his assailants.

Ripon: The city hornblower sounds a forest horn in the market square every night at 9pm. This is the signal that the Wakeman has taken charge of the city for the night.

Beverley: Was known as the "City of Refuge" as it was one of Britain's greatest sanctuaries for hundreds of years. A registry of fugitives stated that from 1478-1539, 439 people sought perpetual immunity, including 186 guilty of manslaughter or homicide.

Sowerby Bridge: Rushbearing is a September ceremony, revived in 1977. The original purpose of rushbearing was to cover the floors of the local churches.

Hawes: Another recently revived annual festival takes place near Hawes – the Hardraw Force Brass Band Festival. However, it's a recital with a difference as it takes place in a natural amphitheatre by Hardraw Force Waterfall.

Hebden Bridge: The Pace Egg Play is performed around Hebden Bridge on Good Friday by the boys of Calder High School – the Midgley version of a traditional play.

Brighouse: Brighouse Children's Theatre perform the Brighouse version of the Pace Egg Play on Easter Saturday.

Birthplaces of the Famous

Bradford: Frederick Delius, composer. David Hockney, painter, stage designer and photographer. Born in 1937, he now lives in California. J. B. Priestley, born at 34 Mannheim Road on September 13th, 1894.

Wakefield: It's claimed that Robin Hood was born here. The local court roll records state details of proceedings conducted against him when, as a youth, he stole firewood.

Thirsk: In 1755, Thomas Lord, founder of Lord's cricket ground.

Castleford: Henry Moore, sculptor, in 1898. He died in 1986 and had been awarded the Order of Merit for his contribution to the world of art.

Thornton: At 74 Market Street between 1816 and 1819, the Bronte sisters who later moved to Haworth.

Pontefract: Dick Turpin, 17th century highwayman. He was said to have driven from Gravesend to York in a day.

Otley: Thomas Chippendale, famous furniture-maker.

Morley: H.H. Asquith, P.M.

York: In 1570, Guy Fawkes.

Birstall: In 1733, Joseph Priestley, "Father of modern chemistry".

Knaresborough: John Metcalfe, better known as "Blind Jack". Although he went blind at the age of six as the result of smallpox, he became a famous road and bridge builder and laid down 180 miles of road in all. At one time he had 400 men working for him.

Selby: Henry I, fourth son of the Conqueror and his only English-born son.

Who Said That?

King George V said that the history of York is the history of England.

Barnsley was once described by Wesley as "a place famous for all manner of wickedness!"

Charles Dickens in 1858 described Harrogate as "the queerest place, with the strangest people in it, leading the oddest lives".

Harrogate used to be known as "The Queen of the Watering Places".

A ghostly lady in white appeared at Bolling Hall, Bradford saying "Pity poor Bradford".

It's a Fact...

The Lord Mayor of York is entitled to be addressed as "My Lord" only during his term of office, but his wife can insist on being called "My Lady" for life.

During the Black Death which hit Yorkshire in 1349, in York alone a third of the population perished.

VILLAGES AND HAMLETS

Most northerly settlement: Redcar.

Most southerly settlement: Totley, near Sheffield.

Most easterly settlement: Kilnsea, on the Spurn Peninsula.

Most westerly settlement: Low Bentham, near Ingleton.

Highest village: Greenhow Hill (1,250 ft.), between Grassington and Pateley Bridge.

Remotest village: Kettleness about 6 miles from Whitby. The nearest bus stop is 1½ miles away. Walden lies nearly 6 miles from the village of West Burton.

Highest maypole: Barwick, near Leeds, 95 feet. The maypole weighs about two tons and the base is about 6 feet below the level of the village square.

Narrowest street: Dog Laup, Staithes, about 20 inches wide.

Longest single-word place name: Sutton-under-Whitestonecliffe, North Yorkshire. 27 letters, although sometimes "the" is added and the "e" is dropped, giving 29.

Strangest Place Names

Booze: In the hills above Langthwaite, Booze is a hamlet with no pub.

Giggleswick: doesn't have anything to do with sniggering – it was the "wic" or village of a Scandinavian Chief called Gigel.

Wales: can be found in Yorkshire! Wales is one of the southernmost villages near the Derbyshire border.

Claims To Fame (to name but a few!)

Goathland: A two-week holiday here was a prize on TV's "Sale of the Century".

Healaugh, near Tadcaster: The original Derby and Joan were said to have lived here.

Kilburn, between Thirsk and Helmsley: Overlooked by the famous white horse of Roulston Scar. The horse was first made by a local schoolmaster and his class in 1857. The ground was coated with lime to keep the horse white, although many other methods have been tried and tested since.

Brompton by Sawdon: It was here that William Wordsworth married Mary Hutchinson of Gallows Hill Farm in 1802.

Appletreewick: The Lord Mayor of London, William Craven was born in one of its cottages in 1549.

Cowthorpe (see "Trees"): Could also boast that Guy Fawkes was once a bellringer at the church.

Croft Spa: Lewis Carroll was the rector's son and it was here that he drew his inspiration for "*Alice in Wonderland*".

Dalby-cum-Skewsby: Has a rare turf maze, the only one of its kind in the country.

Lillings Ambo (the parish title for East and West Lilling): During excavations there, a 13th century village was discovered.

Scorton (See "Traditional Competitive Events"): Has the only walled village green.

Best-Kept Villages

Competitions for the best-kept village in Yorkshire are sponsored by the Yorkshire Rural Community Council. Winning villages, which are presented with an oak seat by *The Dalesman*, have been:-

1959   Carperby, Wensleydale
1961   Bishop Burton, near Beverley
1962   Appleton-le-Moors, near Pickering
1963   Burnsall, Wharfedale
1964   Sledmere, near Malton

1965	Kirkby Overblow, near Harrogate; Cropton, near Pickering
1966	Waddington, near Clitheroe; Wath, near Ripon
1967	Howsham, near Malton; Green Moor, near Penistone
1968	Ramsgill, Nidderdale; Coxwold, near Thirsk
1969	Long Preston, near Settle; Kirkby Fleetham, near Northallerton
1970	Bishop Burton; Cawthorn, near Barnsley
1971	West Ayton, near Scarborough; Roecliffe, near Boroughbridge
1972	Long Preston; Ainderby Steeple, near Northallerton
1973	Langton, near Malton; Hooton Pagnell, near Doncaster
1974	Sicklinghall, near Wetherby; Welburn, near Malton
1975	Snape, near Bedale; Thornton-in-Craven
1976	Lund, near Driffield; Cawthorn
1977	Dishforth, near Ripon; Barton le Willows, near Malton; West Bretton, near Kirkburton
1978	Coxwold, near Thirsk; Aldbrough St John, near Richmond
1979	Hooton Pagnell; Burley-in-Wharfedale, near Otley
1980	Follifoot, near Harrogate; Cloughton, near Scarborough
1981	Carlton in Cleveland; Austwick, near Settle
1982	Letwell, near Maltby; Kildwick, near Skipton
1983	Bishopmonkton, near Ripon; Aislaby, Whitby
1984	Sessay, near Thirsk; Bainbridge, Wensleydale
1985	Hooton Pagnell; Thorner, near Leeds
1986	Masham, near Ripon; Sandsend, near Whitby
1987	Thornton-in-Craven, West Tanfield
1988	Cawthorne, Thorner
1989	Claxton, Menwith-with-Darley
1990	Carlton-in-Cleveland, Bolton Abbey
1991	Collingham, Micklethwaite

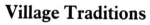

Village Traditions

Egton Bridge, near Whitby: Has an annual gooseberry show which attracts fierce competition as well as numerous sightseers. Egton Bridge Old Gooseberry Society was formed in 1800.

West Witton, near Leyburn: Has an annual tradition of burning Owd Bartle, some say supposedly a straw effigy of St Bartholomew who was said to have been burned at the stake about four hundred years ago, others claim it commemorates an 18th century pig rustler.

Bainbridge: Every night at nine o'clock from September 28 to Shrovetide in February, a three foot long horn is blasted three times by a member of the Metcalfe family. Its original purpose was to guide travellers through the forest, although the forest has long since vanished.

Charter For Success

Helmsley was a borough as early as the end of the twelfth century. According to "A History of Helmsley, Rievaulx and District" written by the members of the Helmsley and Area Group of the Yorkshire Archeological Society and edited by J. McDonnell, M.A., B.Litt., "It is indeed remarkable that very little more than a hundred years after the wasting of this area by William the Conqueror in 1069 there should have been enough prosperity in the town to have enabled a borough charter to be granted".

That there was a growing prosperity was evident by the various trades and crafts in the town including "smiths, millers, a thresher, a tailor, a comber of wool, dyers, tanners, a man who keeps ploughs, a reaper, a cowherd, a mower, coopers, cooks, and a baker".

The prices for the various animals and crops at that time were as follows – cows, 3s. 10d.; sheep, 7d.; pigs 1s.; hay was 10d. a cartload; oats, 7½d. per quarter and the best wheat 2s. 10d. per quarter.

Later on, weaving became a notable industry and there were reputed to be no less than 26 ale-houses in the town as "the weavers were thirsty souls" and beer could be sold "all round the clock".

THE LIE OF THE LAND
The Coast

Total length from Tees to Spurn Point: 117 miles.

Highest sea cliff: Boulby Cliff – 666ft. (Highest point on the East Coast of England).

First Yorkshire pier: Hornsea, Pier Company, 1865. It was 1,072ft. long and cost £10,680. It survived for fifteen years.

Mountains and Moorland

Principal summits over 2,200 feet:

	Feet	Nearest community
Whernside	2,414	Chapel-le-Dale
Ingleborough	2,373	Ingleton
Great Shunner Fell	2,340	Hawes
High Seat	2,328	Mallerstang (Cumbria)
Great Whernside	2,310	Kettlewell
Buckden Pike	2,302	Buckden
Penyghent	2,273	Horton-in-Ribblesdale
Hugh Seat	2,257	Mallerstang (Cumbria)
Lovely Seat	2,213	Hawes
Widdale Fell	2,203	Hawes
Rogan's Seat	2,203	Keld

All the above summits are part of the Yorkshire Pennines.

The highest points elsewhere in Yorkshire are:

South Yorkshire	– Black Hill	1,908	near Holmfirth
North York Moors	– Urra Moor	1,489	Bilsdale
East Yorkshire	– Garrowby Hill	807	Bishop Wilton

Rivers and Lakes

Yorkshire has 3,556 miles of main river

Longest water course: From the source of the River Swale to Spurn Point, below Hull, is 184 miles.

Shortest river: River Bain, 2½ miles from Semerwater to its confluence with the River Ure.

Lengths of other Yorkshire rivers in miles (the Ribble is excluded because it is shared between Yorkshire and Lancashire):

RIVER	NON-TIDAL LENGTH	TIDAL LENGTH	TOTAL
Aire	72½	15½	88
Swale	83	–	83
Wharfe	71	9½	80½
Derwent	75	–	75
Don	52¾	19¼	72
Ure	68½	–	68½
Nidd	60	–	60
Ouse	18	39	57
Calder	51¾	–	51¾
Hull	10	19	29
Esk	21½	2½	24

Drainage area of Yorkshire rivers (in square miles)

Derwent	722	Ure	389
Don	669	Ouse	370
Swale	567	Calder	366
Aire	429	Nidd	211
Wharfe	390	Esk	140

Only river on which it is possible to canoe from the source: The Aire at Malham.

Furthest point inland reached by salmon: The Leyburn area on the Ure and Westerdale on the Esk.

Lake with neither feeder nor outlet: Gormire, near Sutton Bank, North Yorkshire.

Largest natural sheet of water: Hornsea Mere, 467 acres.

Last remnant of a glacial lake in Yorkshire:
Semerwater, in Wensleydale. Legend says that a town lies at the bottom of the lake as a result of a witch's curse.

Highest earth-filled dam (in Britain): Scammonden 242 feet which is unique in being crossed by a motorway (the M62).

Highest surface fall of unbroken water: Hardraw Force, c100 feet. An intrepid soul named Blondin walked over it on a tightrope and cooked an omelette at the same time!

Oldest river conservancy: The Ouse, established in 1305 and confirmed by Charter of Edward IV in 1462.

Most inland port: Selby, 66 miles from the North Sea.

Caves and Potholes

Deepest pothole: Meregill Hole, Chapel-le-Dale, 560 feet (if the terminal sump in Black Shiver Pot, Chapel-le-Dale, can be negotiated, the depth of this pothole would be 640 feet. The sump is 200 feet long and emerges at the upstream end of the Torrent in Meregill Hole).

Deepest underground pitch: Nick Pot, Ingleborough Allotment, 328 feet. An alternative route leads to the top of the main shaft instead of the original route which led to the shaft part-way down. Discovered by University of Leeds Speleological Association, 1972. Also sports the most stupendous underground traverse in Britain –60 feet long above a drop of 250 feet.

Deepest pitch: Gaping Gill main shaft – 365 feet from moor level, 340 feet from stream bed. Usually descended by winch. Also claims to have highest unbroken waterfall in country, though that which falls over the lip of the shaft is broken by a ledge 190 feet down. An unbroken waterfall, 320 feet deep, enters the main shaft via Spout Tunnel.

Most extensive system: Gaping Gill/Ingleborough Cave, whose length of explored and surveyed passages now exceeds 10 miles.

Most severe system: Generally regarded as Langcliffe Pot, near Conistone, Upper Wharfedale. Length 6 miles, depth 380 feet.

Tightest negotiable crawl: Black Shiver Pot, Chapel-le-Dale (7 inches, roof to floor, 50 per cent air, 50 per cent water).

Largest single underground cavity: Gaping Gill main chamber. It is 460 feet long, 110 feet high, and 90 feet wide.

Cave system at which the largest number of rescues have been carried out: Dow Cave, Kettlewell, mostly in Dowbergill Passage which links with alternative entrance at Providence Pot.

National Parks

North Yorkshire has two National Parks – the Yorkshire Dales and the North York Moors. In addition, a small part of the Peak District National Park falls within the boundaries of South Yorkshire.

Yorkshire Dales National Park:

Area: 680 square miles.

Number of people living in the Park: 19,858 in 83 parishes (1987).

Visitors annually: Approximately 8.5 million (7.25 million from April-October).

Visitors on a typical summer Sunday: 60,000.

Visitors to the six National Park Information Centres: 477,000 (in 1990), April-October.

Cars and coaches annually: 425,000 cars and 4,500 coaches (1985).

Day visitors: 62% (80% in 1975).

Staying visitors: 38% (20% in 1975).

First-time visitors: 26%

People taking a walk of over three miles: Approximately two million.

"Three Peaks": Number climbing Ingleborough – up to 120,000; Penyghent – 90,000, Whernside – 50,000; and attempting the Three Peaks Walk – 15,000.

Talks, film shows, walks given to school groups: 1,140 in 1988. Of these, 80% were for visiting schools, 20% local.

Postal requests annually for information: 2,050.

Farmer holdings: About 1,200.

Annual net expenditure 1989/90: £1,524,000.

Percentage of the Park which is common land: 28% (190.4 square miles).

Percentage of land rented: 49.5%.

Percentage of land owner occupied: 51.5%.

Land use:

from Countryside Commission Project "Maintaining Landscape Change".

Cultivated land	72 hectares – 0.04%
Broadleaved woodland	2441 hectares – 1.38%
Coniferous woodland	4750 hectares – 2.69%
Grassland	71,735 hectares – 40.55%
Rough grazing	95,281 hectares – 53.87%
Open water	347 hectares – 0.20%
Other	2241 hectares – 1.27%

North York Moors National Park:

Area: 553 square miles.

Length of coastline: 26 miles. (Boulby to Burniston).

Cliff erosion: An estimated 2 inches per year.

People living in the Park: 25,960. (1988)

Visitor days: approximately 11 million p.a.

Miles of public footpaths and bridleways: 1,130 miles, approx.

Acreage of reservoirs and lakes: 213½ acres.

Railways: British Rail – Esk Valley line (Middlesbrough-Whitby) 35 miles. North Yorks Moors Historical Railway Trust (Grosmont-Pickering) 18 miles.

Visitors to National Park Centres (1990/91): Moors Centre, Danby – 89,592, Sutton Bank Information Centre – 120,337.

Staff: 62 full time and 23 part time (1991).

Voluntary Rangers: 127.

Budget: £1,982,000 (April 1991).

Land Use

Heather moorland and unimproved grazing: 35%.

Woodland and forest area: 22%.

Farmland and other habitats: 43%.

Percentage of Park in private ownership: Over 80%.

National Nature Reserve: Forge Valley, 156 acres, owned by Scarborough Borough Council.

Number of sites of Special Scientific Interest: 54 sites, covering 5,965 hectares (14,739 acres).

NATURAL HISTORY

Oldest nature reserve: Established at Walton Hall, near Wakefield, by Charles Waterton, an outstanding Yorkshire naturalist.

Trees

Largest forest: The North Riding Forest Park, part of the Forestry Commission North York Moors Forest District has an area of 12,220 hectares of forest. There is a further 16,360 hectares of Forestry Commission and Private Estate woodland in the Forest District.

First trees to appear in Yorkshire: Birch, followed by hazel, pine, elm, oak and alder.

Oldest tree: At Cowthorpe, near Marston Moor, is the dead remnants of the Cowthorpe Oak, a sapling during the Roman occupation. For many generations it was the oldest living thing in Britain.

Tallest tree: A lime tree at Duncombe Park, Helmsley, measures 150ft.

Greatest private tree planting: First Baron Ribblesdale, Gisburne Park. The trees planted included 1,200,000 oaks.

First Ribston Pippin apple tree: At Ribston Hall, near Knaresborough. Of three pips introduced, only one developed satisfactorily.

Flowers:

Rarest plant: Lady's Slipper Orchid (Cypripedium calceolus). Clings tenaciously to a small secret spot in the dales. A Mistress Tomalin bragged about stripping Helks Wood, near Ingleton, of this plant. She incurred the wrath of Reginald Farrer.

Largest botanical garden: Bradford, Lister Park, 53 acres.

Animals

Largest wild mammal: Red deer, found in North Yorkshire.

Smallest wild mammal: Pigmy shrew.

Largest carnivore: The badger is the largest in Britain, an average adult boar weighing just under 30lbs. One of 60lbs was killed near Rotherham in the winter of 1952.

Greatest escape: A cat, being pursued by a dog in Bradford in 1980, made a bid for freedom by shinning up the sheer face of a five-storey block of flats – a height of 70ft.

Most elderly pet mouse: A pet mouse called Dixie, owned by A. Newton of Sheffield, lived to the ripe old age of 6½ years. Dixie died in 1981.

Largest litter: An Irish setter by the name of "Settrina Baroness Medina" beat the British record in 1974 by giving birth to 22 puppies, 15 of the litter surviving. She was owned by Mgr. M.J. Buckley of Wetherby.

Speediest tortoise: The record is held by "Charlie" who, at Tickhill on 2nd July, 1977, attained the breakneck speed of 18ft. up a 1:12 gradient in 43.7 seconds.

Most amazing animal discoveries: The remains of hippopotamus have been found at Armley, Leeds; rhinoceros, lions and elephants at Kirkdale Cave, Kirkby Moorside; and mammoth and bison at Sewerby, near Bridlington.

Unluckiest animal: If Whitby fishermen see a pig on the way to their boats, they believe it to be so unlucky, they won't put to sea.

Birds

Most recent bird colonists: Collared dove, little ringed plover, fulmar petrel. A Temminck's Stint laid eggs (but did not hatch them out) near Leeds.

Largest bird of prey: Buzzard, in the north-west of Yorkshire.

Smallest bird: Goldcrest.

Largest concentration of sea birds: Flamborough and Bempton Cliffs.

Only mainland nesting haunt of gannet in England: Bempton Cliffs.

Largest roost: Fairburn Ings, near Pontefract, used in autumn migration by swallows and sand martins (c250,000 birds).

Weather and Climate

Severest winter within living memory: 1947. It began on February 2nd and was especially severe on the Pennines.

Flood disasters: The worst flood disaster occurred at Sheffield on March 12th, 1864, when the Dale Dyke Dam, near Bradfield, burst after heavy rain. 114 million cubic feet of water tore down the Loxley and Don valleys, drowning 260 people and 693 animals and destroying 15 bridges and 100 buildings.

Holmfirth, famous as the location of BBC TV's "Last of The Summer Wine" also suffered a flood disaster on February 5th, 1852 when a wall of water 18-24 feet high swept through the town and killed about a hundred people. It also destroyed four mills, eight bridges, ten warehouses, 18 barns and 27 cottages.

Other severe floods causing serious damage occurred in Wharfedale in 1673, Helmsley (Ryedale) in 1754, Yarm in 1771, Hardraw Scar (Wensleydale) in 1899, Eskdale in 1930 and 1931, Littondale in 1953, and Swaledale in 1986 ("Hurricane Charlie").

Heaviest recorded rainfall: Possibly the 190½ inches at Ribblehead in 1954 (average about 70 inches). There was a rainfall of 5.2 inches on December 2nd that year.

Some Yorkshire Toasts

The Lord be thanked for what we've getten.
If ther'd been more to eit ther'd hev been more etten.

★ ★ ★

Here's health to thee an' thine, likewise to me an' mine.
When thee an' thine cum to see me an' mine, me an' mine
will try an' mak thee an' thine as happy as thee an' thine med
me an' mine when me an' mine cum to see thee an' thine.

★ ★ ★

Here's to you, as good as you are,
Here's to me, as bad as I am,
As bad as I am and as good as you are,
I'm as good as you, as bad as I am.

★ ★ ★

Here's tiv him be he Tyke or
Foreigner wheea can truly say
He war nivver maesthered
By owther hoss or woman.

★ ★ ★

The following verse (not actually a toast), was said when a
man was about to drink a glass of beer:

Oft times tha's made me pawn mi clothes,
Oft times tha's made mi friends to foes,
But now tha's here afore mi nose,
Up tha pops and dahn tha goes.

FARMING AND AGRICULTURE

Livestock

Largest heifer: Craven heifer, born 1897. It was reared by the Rev. William Carr at Bolton Abbey, Wharfedale. Girth in the middle 10ft. 2 inches; at the loin 9ft. 11 inches; height at shoulder 5ft. 2 inches; length from nose to rump 11ft. 2 inches.

Largest pig: Bred at Rillington, near Malton (according to "Yorkshire Magazine" for March 1876). Weighed 51 stones 11 pounds.

First Large White Pig: Bred by a Keighley weaver named Tuley, in 1851.

Oldest pedigree poultry farm: Snowdens, of Cowling.

Largest hen egg: Weighed 8½ ounces. Laid by a hen owned by Peter Quarton, Lodge Farm, Kexby Bridge, near York, in March 1964.

First hackney pony to be exhibited: Sired by a horse named Sportsman, which was of Yorkshire blood, about 1866.

Machinery and Shows

First grass drier: Operated at The Grange, Carleton, near Skipton, about 1928.

First helicopter used to spray land with chemicals: At the Bolton Estate, Wensleydale, in 1959, when an area of bracken-infested land was treated.

Largest cattle shed: At the Yorkshire Agricultural Society's permanent showground at Harrogate. The shed is 456 feet long and can accommodate 686 cows, all in separate stalls. There are also boxes for two bulls.

Earliest agricultural show: Otley. It was established in 1796. For about 12 years before that, farmers organized shows for £1 wagers in an Otley inn yard.

Largest show: Great Yorkshire, held in July at a permanent showground at Harrogate. A three day event. The Yorkshire Agricultural Society organized its first show in 1837.

The Beginning ... and The End

At Wakefield the Zoological Gardens were opened on July 10th, 1839, by a Mr. Russell. They contained artificial rocks and terraces, wild animals, collections of shells and insects from China, baths and instrumental music. Half a guinea was the cost of a yearly ticket, or a guinea covered a family of five.

Unfortunately, the zoo's existence was short lived. Five years after it opened, a bear climbed a pole in the bear pit and escaped. It inflicted injuries upon a Mrs Haslegrave, who lived within the gardens and she unfortunately died about a week later. The bear was shot. The zoo was afterwards closed through lack of public support.

TRANSPORT AND COMMUNICATIONS
Roads

Highest roads (over 1,500 feet):	ft.
Fleet Moss (Buckden to Hawes)	1,934
The Fleak (Askrigg to Reeth)	1,785
Tan Hill (Arkengarthdale to Brough)	1,753
Buttertubs (Hawes to Muker)	1,726
Holme Moss (Holmfirth to Woodhead A.6024)	1,718
Lamps Moss (Keld to Kirkby Stephen B.6270)	1,698
Stang (Arkengarthdale to Barnard Castle)	1,677
Park Rash (Kettlewell to Coverdale)	1,652
Oxnop Head (Askrigg to Muker)	1,633
White Moss (Holmfirth to Greenfield A.635)	1,615
White Shaw Moss (Kingsdale to Dent)	1,553
Grinton Moor (Redmire to Grinton)	1,523

Except for the three numbered roads listed above, all are unclassified.

Steepest road: Rosedale Bank Top, North Yorkshire. Maximum gradient 1 in 3.

Highest motorway (in Britain): M62 at Windy Hill on West Yorkshire/Lancashire border (1,220 feet).

Deepest roadway cutting (in Europe): Deanhead Cutting on M62.

First Yorkshire turnpike act: 1735, covering the roads from Manchester and Oldham to Saddleworth, and from Rochdale over Blackstone Edge to Halifax and Elland.

Oldest milestone: Lilla Cross, North York Moors, believed to date back 1,300 years.

Most informative milestone: Possibly the four-direction stone at the junction of Skipton to Colne and Elslack and Cross Hills road. Dated 1730.

31

Longest single-span bridge (in Britain): At Deanhead (410 feet), carrying the A.6025 over the M63.

Longest single-span suspension bridge (in the world): The Humber Bridge (4,626 feet), opened by HM the Queen in July 1981.

Largest vertical lift bridge (in the world): Middlesbrough. Opened on February 28th, 1934.

Only double-arched bridge: East Marton, between Skipton and Gisburn. The lower bridge was built over the Leeds and Liverpool canal prior to 1770. Another bridge was built above it for the road.

Oldest toll bridge: Selby. When the bridge was opened to traffic in 1791, a right was granted as a local concession under the Bridge Act of George III and it still applies. The bridge is 75 yards long and 20 feet 6 inches wide, and was substantially rebuilt in 1970-71.

First public stage coach: 1658, from York to London, a journey of four days.

First Leeds–London Royal Mail Coach: 1785, a journey of 26 hours.

Oldest fire engine: Kept at Knaresborough Castle.

First tramways: Horse-drawn rail cars at Leeds in 1872.

First electric trams (in England): The first operated from overhead wires on a commercial basis were in 1891 at Leeds on the Sheepscar-Oakwood route.

First dual-gauge tramcars: At Leeds in 1907. They connected the tramway systems at Leeds (4 feet 8½ inches) and Bradford (4 feet).

Oldest surviving tramcar (in Britain): In the Transport and Archaeology Museum in Hull.

First trolley buses: Trial installation by Leeds in conjunction with Bradford in 1911.

First motor bus: Todmorden, 1907, although it has been suggested that Ezra Laycock of Barnoldswick may have had one at an even earlier date.

First motor cabs: Northern Motor Cab Company Ltd., Bradford, in 1908.

First British firm to sell motor cars on H.P.: Yorkshire Motor Car Co. in 1897.

First car hire service in Britain: From J.E. Tuke in 1896, you could have hired a two-seater "Sociable" for three shillings an hour or a six-seater "Victoria" for £10 a month.

First motor agent: J.E. Tuke of Harrogate and Bradford. He was agent for Arnold Motor carriages in October 1896.

First doctor to use a motor car: Dr. T. Pritchard Roberts of Harrogate.

Canals

Highest point on a Yorkshire canal: Just under 500 feet near Salterforth on the Leeds-Liverpool canal, 1792. The closed Huddersfield Narrow Canal reached approximately 650 feet at Standedge.

Longest canal tunnel: Standedge, Huddersfield Narrow Canal, which has a length of 3 miles, 135 yards. It was closed in 1944.

Longest canal "pound": Bingley Five Rise on the Leeds-Liverpool canal. It alters the height of the water by 59 feet 2 inches.

Canal with largest number of locks: Leeds and Liverpool with over 90 locks. There is a flight of 21 on the Lancashire side.

Longest possible journey on Britain's canal system: From Bedford on the Great Ouse to near Ripon, North Yorkshire (415¾ miles, 157 locks).

Railways

First railway to be authorised by Parliament (in Britain): Middleton Railway, Leeds, constructed under Act of 9 June 1758. Opened in the same year as a wooden waggonway. Converted in 1811 to become the first rack railway in the world.

First locomotives to be used commercially on a flanged rail (in the world): "Salamanca" and "Prince Regent", designed and built by Matthew Murray at the Round Foundry, Water Lane, Holbeck, Leeds. They went into regular service on the Middleton Railway on August 12th, 1812. A portion of the railway is still in use, preserved by the Middleton Railway Trust. Steam locomotives are still at work after 175 years – a world record.

First steam-worked public railway: Leeds & Selby Railway, opened 22nd September 1834. The line left Leeds through Richmond Hill tunnel, the first in the world through which passengers were drawn by a locomotive. To minimise passenger hysteria, it was whitewashed and copper plates were installed at the foot of air shafts to reflect light!

Shortest independent railway: Easingwold Railway, extending for 2½ miles from the East Coast main line at Alne. Open from 1891 to 1957.

Only municipally-owned public railway (in Britain): Bradford Corporation's Nidd Valley Light Railway, open for passengers from 1907 to 1929.

Highest summit: The Incline Top on the Battersby to Rosedale mineral line was approximately 1,350 feet above sea-level. The highest summit still in use is on the Settle-Carlisle railway at Ais Gill on the border with Cumbria – 1,167 feet. This is also the highest main line railway summit in England.

Highest station: Ribblehead, 1,020 feet – on the Settle-Carlisle line.

Highest stone viaduct: Lockwood (136 feet) on the Huddersfield-Penistone line. The now demolished Staithes viaduct (152 feet) on the Whitby-Loftus line was the highest metal viaduct.

Longest tunnel: Totley – 3 miles 950 yards – running from Grindleford in Derbyshire to Dore and Totley in Yorkshire. The original Woodhead tunnel was 3 miles 22 yards long and the new tunnel has a length of 3 miles 66 yards. The longest tunnel wholly in Yorkshire is Bramhope – 2 miles 241 yards – on the Leeds-Harrogate line.

Highest tunnel: Shotlock Hill, south of Ais Gill summit, on the Settle-Carlisle railway, at an altitude of approx. 1,153 ft.

Deepest cutting (in Britain): At Chevet, near Wakefield, on the Midland main line – almost 100 feet deep.

Steepest incline to carry passenger traffic: The rope-worked Beck Hole incline on the Whitby-Pickering line, 1 in 10. It carried passengers from 1836 to 1865.

Longest straight stretch of track (in Britain): 18 miles between Barlby and Staddlethorpe on the Selby-Hull line.

Only railway to run through a roundabout: The now dismantled Catterick Camp Military Railway, which intersected a roundabout at a road junction.

Longest station platform: York, platform 8 (1,692ft).

Longest station seat (in the world): Scarborough – a continuous wooden seat 285ft. long along the base of a retaining wall on Platform 1.

Fastest speed with diesel traction: Recorded on 12 June 1973 when the prototype Inter-City 125 High Speed Train attained 143mph between Northallerton and Thirsk.

Air

First balloon flight: Mr Lunardi, from Leeds in 1785.

First air service: The Great Yorkshire Show Airline between Leeds and Bradford in 1914. The aircraft was a monoplane made in Leeds by the Blackburn Aeroplane Company Ltd.

Slowest aircraft (in the world): The amphibious Camco V-liner 52 mph. Built for the Central Aircraft Manufacturing Company by the Slingsby Aircraft Company at Kirkbymoorside.

First solo flight to Australia: Amy Johnson of Hull in 1930.

First aeroplane: A 5ft. glider completed in 1804 by Sir George Cayley, "Father of Aviation". He was born in Scarborough and his private workshop was at Brompton Hall, the family seat.

First "successful" test flight in a man-carrying glider: In 1853, John Appleby, Cayley's coachman, "volunteered" to fly across a valley near Brompton Hall. After the 500 yard flight, he left Cayley's employment – presumably to escape the possibility of being asked to execute an action replay!

First aviation meeting: At Doncaster in 1909 where Delagrange broke the world speed record by exceeding a breathtaking 53 miles an hour.

First flying club: Yorkshire Light Aeroplane Club held its inaugural meeting at Hotel Metropole, Leeds on the 15th September, 1909. Within a month, the membership was over 200.

First aerodrome: Airedale Aerodrome sited at Rawdon Meadows, actually part of Esholt Sewage Works Estate!

First successful aircraft building enterprise: Founded by Robert Blackburn, born in Leeds on 26th March, 1885. A complete aircraft in 1910 would have set you back around £700.

Oldest (British) flyable aircraft: Blackburn monoplane of 1912.

Most persistant "trier": Probably Richard "Bobby" Allen, the flying policeman of Bradford. He was of the firm belief that if he pedalled hard enough, his cycle fitted with wings would eventually fly. It didn't.

First woman parachute jump: 1906 at Haworth. Unfortunately, it was fatal. She jumped from a balloon near Ponden reservoir and her parachute failed.

Sea Facts

Oldest lifeboat (in the world): Redcar, 1800. It was in service at Spurn until 1802 then brought to Redcar and rechristened *Zetland*. In 60 years of service she saved over 500 lives.

During Whitby's whale fishing in the Eighteenth Century, over 3,000 whales were landed.

Only lighthouse in the middle of a residential street: At Withernsea. It can be reached by stepping off the pavement. The houses have been built around it.

INDUSTRY

Iron and Steel

First forge: In 1161, worked by the monks of Kirkstead, at Kimberworth under a grant made by Richard de Busli, Lord of the Manor of Sheffield.

Oldest forge: Kirkstall, started by Kirkstall monks in 1200. Financially controlled by the same family since 1779.

First fused plating: Invented by Thomas Boulsover, Sheffield. c. 1740.

First crucible steel: Benjamin Huntsman, at Sheffield, c.1740.

Oldest saw-makers: Spear and Jackson, Sheffield, 1760.

Longest wire rope ever spun in one piece: British Ropes Ltd., Doncaster, 46,653 feet (8.83 miles), $3\frac{1}{8}$ inches circumference, weight $28\frac{1}{2}$ tons.

Discovery of stainless steel: Sheffield 1913.

Smallest knife: Half inch long, made in Sheffield.

Oldest cutlery manufacturing firm: Joseph Rodgers & Sons Ltd. Granted its trademark in 1683 and responsible for the penknife with the greatest number of blades in the world. The knife was built in 1822 with 1822 blades.

First private mark granted to a cutler: William Elles in 1554.

Mining

Largest single coalfield (in England): Yorkshire, producing 26 million tonnes, 30% of the nation's coal.

Oldest working colliery in the Yorkshire coalfield: Houghton Main, near Barnsley. Originally sunk in 1860.

First practical steam engine: A Newcomen engine, Garrowtree Pit, Kimberworth, near Rotherham, then part of the estates of the Marquess of Rockingham, 1823.

First church bells in a coal mine: 1904, Horserigg Colliery, Gilderstone, by ringers of St James' Church, Bolton, Bradford.

Largest amount of saleable coal ever won in Yorkshire in a single year: 46.5 million tons in 1924. The largest coal mine now working is Kellingley, Knottingley, producing more than two million tonnes a year.

Deepest shaft: North Selby, 1008 metres. The mine is 6 miles S.E. of York.

Highest productivity: Stillingfleet Mine near Selby. The mine set up a British productivity record of 30.36 tonnes a man shift in March 1991.

Fastest mine sinking: 102.4 metres in 31 days (January 1961) – No. 2 Shaft at Kellingley Colliery, Knottingley.

Longest Conveyor: 12.3 km at Gascoigne Wood, making a total belt of 24.6 km.

Power

First power loom: At Doncaster, 1787 (Edmund Cartwright's loom was tried).

First use of steam power in a mill: 1798, Holme Mill, Bradford, by Ramsbottom, Swaine and Murgatroyd.

Largest waterwheel: Lotherdale, James Wilson & Son, Ltd., 48 feet diameter and 70 h.p., installed before 1849.

Power Station with greatest capacity: Ferrybridge "C" 2,000 M.W.

Highest chimney: Drax, near Selby, completed 1971. The largest capacity stack in the world, 850 feet high and 90 feet across.

First gasfield: Found near Whitby in 1937.

Commerce

Oldest Co-operative Society: Leeds.

Oldest retail business: B. Smith Ltd., Thirsk, founded 1580, drapers, furnishers, caterers.

Largest woollen mill: Was Armley Mills, set on an island in the Aire Valley. (Now an industrial museum).

Largest building society (in the world): The Halifax, founded in 1853. Started in a room above a shop in the Old Market, Halifax, at a rent of £10 per year. It has been the largest in the world since 1927. Today, the Halifax employs over 20,000 staff and has over 730 branches, 1,600 agencies and 650 estate agency offices, assets of £54 billion and a savings or borrowing link with 2 in 5 households in the UK.

"The Dalesman"

In April 1939 there appeared a tiny hand-set magazine called *The Yorkshire Dalesman*. Edited by Harry J. Scott, it was written and designed in the front room of his house at Clapham and printing of 4,000 cost £21. A copy was 3d. to buy or, alternatively, a year's subscription cost 3/6d.

The foreword to the first issue was written by J.B. Priestley, wishing the magazine every success for the future – a success which eventually meant remarkable circulation figures. The first company documents were kept in a shoebox, but that shoebox has long since been outgrown – the accounts department now has a computer!

Circulation is now close on 60,000 – the largest of any regional journal in the country and its readership is estimated at five times that figure, as every copy is passed round and read by several people. In other words, Yorkshire folk won't part with their brass for a copy if they can take a sneaky peek for nowt! Overseas subscriptions amount to around 3,000 – and that's not counting the overseas readers who are sent second-hand copies from the folks back home!

The book production side began in 1946, the first being Arthur Raistrick's *The Story of Pennine Wells*, price one shilling. Despite the gloomy prediction of a Yorkshire printer when first faced with the manuscript – "Thou'll noan sell many o' yon" – tens of thousands of copies later, it's still a steady seller! That title is now one of more than 300 in our regional list.

THEATRE, MUSIC AND MEDIA

Theatre

Largest open air theatre: Scarborough. Opened in 1932, it houses a stage 182 feet long and has a seating capacity of 7,000 plus standing room for 9,000.

Oldest theatre: The Georgian Theatre at Richmond is the second oldest in England. Founded in 1788 it's probably also the smallest in Yorkshire. Today it holds 200, although 400 squeezed in on its opening night! The City Varieties Music Hall in Leeds is also a contender for being the oldest theatre. It was a singing room in 1762.

Oldest and largest complete set of painted scenery: 1836, at Richmond.

Music

First Leeds Music Festival: 1858. Also marked the opening of the Town Hall when Queen Victoria visited the city.

Most famous Yorkshire choir: Huddersfield Choral Society, founded in 1832.

Most famous brass bands: Brighouse and Rastrick and Black Dyke Mills.

First Yorkshire brass band contest: Piece Hall, Halifax, over a hundred years ago.

Winners of the first competition: Clayton Band.

Most famous Yorkshire song: "On Ilkla' Moor Baht 'at" – said to have been "invented" by the congregation of a West Riding chapel who were visiting Ilkley on their annual outing. (See page 52).

Media

Oldest newspaper: "The Leeds Mercury" (founded 1718), incorporated in "The Yorkshire Post" in 1939.

First Yorkshire Television broadcast: The Test at Headingley on Monday 29th July, 1968. It was also the first time ITV had ever covered a Test Match live.

The Dales of Yorkshire

It comes as a surprise to many to discover that quite apart from the area known as the Yorkshire Dales – those delectable valleys of the west, some of which are within the Dales National Park – dales occur in all parts of the country. A few years ago, The Dalesman organised a competition through which our readers could discover just how many dales existed. At first consideration, you might list the names of a score, or even a hundred dales. We thought of a figure of about 250. One reader – who at the time had both the inclination and the opportunity for detailed research, using large-scale maps – came up with a staggering 562.

In the east, 16 dales run into one hamlet. Thixendale is the name of this community and the name indeed means "sixteen dales", which are: Waterdale, Williedale, Blubberdale, Courtdale, Honeydale, Buckdale, Longdale, Middledale, Breckondale, Warrendale, Broadholmedale, Pluckamdale, Millandale, Fotherdale, Bowdale and Fairydale.

ARTS AND EDUCATION

Arts

First Ilkley Literature Festival: 1973. Now held biennially, it covers up to eight different events each day.

First sculpture park (first of its kind in the country): Opened at West Bretton, Wakefield in 1977. It covers about 260 acres.

Bram Stoker wrote *Dracula* at Ravenscar.

Charles Kingsley wrote *The Water Babies* at Malham Cove.

(See also "Buildings/Claims to Fame" and "Inns/Claims To Fame").

Education

Earliest comprehensive school: Calder High School, established 1950.

Oldest Roman Catholic school (in England): Bar Convent in York, the oldest continuously existing on the same site.

Oldest school (in England): St Peter's School, York, A.D.627 – claims direct descent from a 7th century grammar school.

First university: Leeds in 1904. It began as the Yorkshire College of Science in 1874 but was granted independent status in 1904.

Sheffield College (1879) was granted university status in the same year (1904).

The Yorkshire Character

The words they use suggest that Yorkshire folk are a very pugnacious breed. If angered, they are likely to *belt, bensill, bray, lace, leather, pawse ('kick')* or *skelp* you.

Again their language suggests that their ranks contain an unfortunate array of idiots. Some are apparently 'as daft as muck' or 'as daft as a scuttle'. Naturally, not all Yorkshire natives are brain-boxes. There was the *lurry drahver* observed frantically trying to claw down the stonework of an arch which his vehicle could not quite pass underneath. 'Why don't you let your tyres down a bit?' asked a helpful passer-by. 'Nay,' answered the stupid driver, 'it's t'lurry roof 'at wain't go under, not t'wheels.'

The Yorkshireman and his dialect are supposedly blunt. Yorkshire people are realistic. 'What an adorable view!' exclaimed a visitor. 'Aye', grunted the dales farmer, 'but it weeant pay t'rent.'

Often, though, bluntness is partly a defence. Under the rough manners and speech lie great kindliness, but you must not show it for fear of looking 'soft'. And far better to qualify a success, so that folk will stay sympathetic towards you. The technique is quite easy. If they ask about your recovery from illness, you reply, 'Ah might just mucky another cleean shirt'; if they congratulate you on your prize flowers, 'Aye, they're middlin', but Ah daht they'll tek a vast lot aht o't'land'; if you win the treble chance, 'Not so bad, but inflation'll sooin wreck it.'

One trouble is that every Yorkshire person has several layers of speech. He won't talk quite the same to the vicar, to a baby, and to a work-mate who drops a paving slab on his toe!

(from *Yorkshire Yammer* by Peter Wright)

BUILDINGS
Homes

First semi-detached houses: Arnford, near Hellifield, a farmhouse built as a pair of semi-detached houses about 1690; probably the first example of such building in England.

Largest municipal block of flats: Quarry Hill, Leeds (938 dwellings set on rather more than three-and-a-half acres).

Largest municipal housing development: Of its time, the Quarry Hill estate in Leeds was the largest in England. Designed in 1935, it occupied about 28 acres and provided homes for over 3000 people.

Highest inhabited building: Apart from Tan Hill, listed here as an inn, the honour goes to Hag Dyke, near Kettlewell (farmhouse now used by Boy Scouts). 1,533 feet above sea level.

Smallest house: Structure on stilts adjoining the west end of All Saints' Church, in North Street, York. One room.

Highest house above ground level: A house in rock beside the Nidd at Knaresborough.

Largest house: Castle Howard, near York. Walpole wrote of this house, designed by Sir John Vanburgh: "Nobody had informed me that at one view I should see a palace, a town, a fortified city". It is now the venue for the Great Yorkshire Steam Fair, held annually.

Longest house: Wentworth Woodhouse, near Barnsley (facade of 600 feet).

Claims to Fame

Sandy Hall, at Coxwold, between York and Thirsk: The place where Laurence Sterne, a local parson wrote *Tristram Shandy* and *Sentimental Journey* around 1760.

Top Withens Farm, past Howarth: said to be the original Earnshaw House in *Wuthering Heights*.

Bronte Parsonage, Haworth: Home of the famous sisters. Now a museum.

Temple Newsam, Leeds: Darnley, husband of Mary Queen of Scots is said to have been born here. The house is also the Templestow of Walter Scott's *Ivanhoe*.

Norton Conyers, a Jacobean House near Ripon: Said to be the original Thornfield House in *Jane Eyre*.

The vicarage at Marton: The definitive "House that Jack built" – it was designed by a man called Jack and the builder and all his men were also named Jack!

Castles

First Roman wooden fortress: York, AD71.

First Norman castle: York, 1069 (wooden). It was believed to have been built in eight days for William of Normandy.

First stone castle: Richmond, c1075.

First keepless castle: Kilton (off the Skelton-Whitby road), 1135-1140.

Oldest round castle keep: Conisbrough, near Doncaster. About 700 years old, 90 feet high.

Largest snow "castle": Settle, 1886. Forty yards in circumference, 15 feet high, crowned by seven turrets. Inside were three chambers, with seating for 60 child diners at a time. While the frost lasted 700 children were fed within its walls and the total number of visitors was 2,000.

Most visited castle: Skipton.

Castle mentioned by Shakespeare: Pontefract, mentioned in Richard III. Richard II was imprisoned and died there.

Only complete roofed castle: Skipton.

Claims to Fame

Bolton Castle: Mary Queen of Scots was once imprisoned there.

Conisbrough Castle: The setting for Walter Scott's *Ivanhoe*.

Churches and Chapels

Oldest church: St. Mary's, Bishophill Junior, York.

Oldest and most complete Saxon church: Kirk Hammerton, nine miles from York.

Oldest complete Saxon tower: Bardsey, near Leeds (800-950 A.D.).

First dissenting place of worship: The original Mill Hill Chapel, Leeds, begun in 1672. It cost £400 and was opened in 1674.

First non-conformist ordination: Pasture House Farm, West Riding, 1678.

Highest parish church: Greenhow Hill, between Grassington (Wharfedale) and Pateley Bridge (Nidderdale). c1,300 feet.

Highest chapel: At Hag Dyke, near Kettlewell (1,533 feet).

First York Minster: When Paulinus baptised King Edwin of Northumbria into Christianity, on Easter Day 627AD. A little wooden church was built on the site.

Largest Gothic cathedral in Nothern Europe: York Minster.

Smallest complete parish church: Speeton, near Bridlington.

Largest church: Most Holy and Undivided Trinity, Kingston-upon-Hull, measuring 288 feet × 124 feet.

Longest church: Warmsworth. The steeple is half a mile from the rest of the building.

Church with loftiest spire: Wakefield Cathedral, 247 feet. Built from 1859 to 1861.

First concrete church: St. John's, Goldthorpe, near Doncaster.

Finest pre-Conquest church tower: Appleton-le-Street, near Malton.

Churches on bridges: Of the three in England, two are in Yorkshire – at Rotherham and Wakefield.

Largest number of churches in one place: York with 18 (41 churches existed up to the Reformation).

Church within a railway station: Doncaster. Going up to London, it is on the left hand side, facing the "engine" after leaving Platform 1.

Oldest octagonal chapel: Heptonstall, the oldest Methodist Chapel in the world in continuous use. The Rev. John Wesley preached there for the last time in 1786.

Church on the site of a pagan temple: Goodmanham Church, East Yorkshire. The temple was destroyed by the pagan priest, Coifi, when he turned to Christianity about 627 AD.

Rev. Patrick Bronte's first church in Yorkshire: Hartshead, near Brighouse.

Largest monastic ruin (in Europe): Fountains Abbey, founded by Cistercian monks in 1132.

Church Furnishings

Oldest furnishing: Frith-stol, or sanctuary chair, at Beverley Minster. It is about 1,000 years old. The seat may have been used by saintly John of Beverley.

Largest stained glass window: Great East Window at York Minster. Dating from early in the 15th century, it is about the size of a tennis court – 78 feet high, 30 feet wide. There is about 1,680 square feet of actual glass.

Olde Bell 1146   Young bells 1087

Oldest stained glass: There are 12th century fragments in the Tree of Jesse in the north aisle of the nave of York Minster.

Oldest bell: Scawton Church. The bell was brought here from Byland Abbey in 1146.

Highest hung peal of bells: Queensbury Church, near Bradford. The church stands at a height of 1,190 feet.

Heaviest ring of 12 bells: York Minster. Total weight of the bells is over 13 tons.

Largest bell (and deepest toned church bell in Europe): Great Peter, York Minster, originally $10\frac{3}{4}$ tons, 8 feet 4 inches in diameter, 7 feet 4 inches high. It was cast in 1845. When recasting took place in 1926 the weight became 10 tons 16 cwt. 22 lb. and the note E-flat. It's rung daily at noon.

First 13 bell ring: Leeds Parish Church, 1841.

Only clock (in the world) to strike on bells in two separate towers: Beverley Minster. It chimes quarters on ten bells in the north tower and the hours on the Big John bell (about seven tons) in the south tower.

The longest clock pendulum (in the country): at Aldborough Parish Church, near Boroughbridge.

Oldest door ring: Adel Church, c700 years old.

Oldest rood loft: Two lofts exist – at Hubberholme, 1588 (Langstrothdale) and Flamborough.

Oldest Sundial: Saxon dial at Kirkdale Church, near Kirkbymoorside. Inscription records the buildings of the church by Orm, son of Gamal, a pre-Conquest overlord.

Finest murals: Pickering. The murals were discovered under whitewash in 1852.

Most inspiring stone carving: Lewis Caroll saw the model of his famous March Hare in a stone carving in St. Mary's church, Beverley.

Most confusing inscription: At Low Bentham a church inscription reads of a woman who became a Husband on her wedding day – Anna Husband! – in 1683.

Inns

Yorkshire has about 3,600 inns – more than any other county in England.

Oldest: The Bingley Arms, Bardsey, near Leeds, restored and extended in 1738, but according to church records, dated 905, it existed as the "Priest's Inn".

Only inn partly within a churchyard: Savile Arms, Church Lane, Thornhill, Dewsbury.

Loneliest: Green Dragon, Hurst, at top of a six-mile cul-de-sac (now closed).

Highest: Tan Hill, on the heights beyond Swaledale, 1,732 feet.

Shortest names: "C.B." Hotel, Arkengarthdale. Ox Inn, Lebberston, near Scarborough.

Longest living fire: In Saltergate Inn, between Pickering and Whitby. Has reputedly been burning for around 200 years.

Claims to Fame

A plaque at the Original Oak Inn at Leeds is made from the wood of an ancient tree where Danish freemen used to assemble around 1,000 years ago. The inn is sited on the same spot.

After Cromwell's victory at Marston Moor in 1644, the wounded were taken to the Sun Inn at Long Marston.

Dick Hudson's on Bingley Moor has a stone marking the place where a gamekeeper was shot by a poacher in 1861.

"Locals" of the famous

Moritt Arms at Gretna Bridge and the **Fleece Inn,** Northallerton: both frequented by Charles Dickens while he was writing *Nicholas Nickleby.*

Rose and Crown, Halifax: it was here that Daniel Defoe wrote part of *Robinson Crusoe.*

Black Bull, Haworth, Branwell Bronte.

Other Buildings

Oldest mental institution: Bootham Park Hospital, York, built 1772.

Deepest well: In St. James's Square, Boroughbridge, 265 feet. It has a canopy supported by eight columns that was built in 1875.

Highest field centre: Malham Tarn House, 1,229 feet above sea level. Run by the Field Studies Council.

First model town: Saltaire, built by Sir Titus Salt, between 1850 and 1870.

Largest folly: Wainhouse Tower at King Cross, near Halifax, 253 feet high; 400 steps to the top.

Tallest self-supported tower (in Great Britain): IBA Transmitter at Emley Moor, West Yorkshire (September 1971). 1080 feet tall, it cost £900,000, has an enclosed room at 865 feet and weighs (with foundations) more than 15,000 tons.

Building containing the longest lift (in the UK): BBC Tower at Bilsdale, West Moor, North Yorkshire (930ft).

Largest radar installation: Fylingdales, completed 1962.

Oldest bank premises: Barclays Bank, Pontefract, opened as bank of Leatham, Tew & Co., 1801.

Oldest pharmacy: E.W. Lawrence, Knaresborough Market Place, founded 1720.

Oldest hall: Probably the Merchant Adventurer's Hall at York (1357).

Only building with sheep grazing on the roof: Marshall Mill on Marshall Street, Leeds, was built about 1840 on the model of an Egyptian Temple and it was rumoured that the owner had a roof garden with sheep grazing on it!

Largest soft drinks factory (in Europe): The Coca-Cola and Schweppes Beverages plant near Leeds. Covering the area of 11 soccer pitches, it required 527,000 tonnes of earth and rock to be excavated, incorporated 20,000 tonnes of steel, more than four miles of drains, two miles of footpaths and provided work for about 7,000 people along the supply line.

Sign Language

The sign at the World's End Inn at Knaresborough showed a coach crashing through the bridge – a reminder of Mother Shipton's prophecy that when the bridge fell three times the world would come to an end.

The Hermit Inn at Burley Woodhead, near Ilkley, pictures the Hermit of Rombalds Moor, Job Senior, who lived on the edge of the moor. In remorse for his wife's death which he believed he had caused, he lived in a kind of dog-kennel on the edge of the moors, eating potatoes roasted on a peat fire.

Yorkshire's "National Anthem"

The famous Yorkshire song, "On Ilkla Moor Baht 'At" is said to have been written in 1886, when a Halifax Church Choir had a summer picnic on Ilkley Moor. During the picnic, a courting couple wandered away from the group – the girl's Christian names were Mary Jane. On their return to the choir party, the famous song originated with the words of the first verse, "Wheear 'as ta been sin' Ah saw thee?" The second verse started with the words "Tha's been a cooartin' Mary Jane."

On the first occasion, the song was sung to the hymn tune Cranbrook, the tune that's still used today.

In the fifties, a team of seventy Soviet singers and dancers sang a Russian translation of the song from the stage of the Drury Lane Theatre:

> *Znai je my videli tebia*
> *On Ilkla Moor baht 'at*
> *Znai je my videli tebia*
> *Znai je my videli tebia*
> *On Ilkla Moor Baht 'at*
> *On Ilkla Moor Baht 'at*
> *On Ilkla Moor Baht 'at*
>
> *Tum ty godials meri jein*
> *On Ilka Moor baht 'at*
> *etc., etc.*

The Yorkshire Post recorded that Mr. Lew Christiansen, the company's director, heard the song from a coach driver when the company was touring the provinces. He translated it – the "baht 'at" defeated him – and it became one of the most rehearsed pieces in the show. Mr. Christiansen was anxious for the company to sing it when they returned to their home town of Sverdlovsk, the most easterly city of European Russia. It was certainly well received in London!

PERSONALITIES
Inventions, Discoveries and "Firsts"

First man to appreciate the properties of oxygen: Joseph Priestley, born at Fieldhead, Birstall, in 1734. He was the discoverer of oxygen.

First maker of liquorice confectionery: George Dunhill, a chemist at Pontefract, 1760.

First wholesale clothier: John Barran, Leeds 1856.

Inventor of "cat's-eyes" reflectors: Percy Shaw of Halifax.

Inventor of a taxi-cab: J.A. Hansom of York.

Inventor of Portland cement: Joseph Aspdin, 1824.

First mass-produced steel pen-nibs: Made by Joseph Gillot, the Sheffield cutler.

First lock, hydraulic press and beer-pump: The creation of Joseph Bramah of Stainborough.

First chronometer: Perfected in 1759 by John Harrison, son of a carpenter at Nostell Priory, thereby revolutionising navigation.

Inventor of the Tonic Sol-fa system: John Curwen of Heckmondwike in 1853.

Founder of Mechanics' Institutes: Dr. George Birbeck of Settle, in 1776.

New translation of the Bible: By Miles Coverdale of Wensleydale in 1526.

The world's first man-carrying glider: Built by Sir George Cayley in 1853. (See "Air"). He lived at Brompton's Wydale Hall and was also a pioneer of the aeroplane, hot air engine, caterpillar tractor and airships.

Founder of the NSPCC: Benjamin Waugh of Settle.

First to use the White Rose as his emblem: Richard Plantagenet, Duke of York.

First Christian missionary after Roman withdrawal: Paulinus, 625.

First Norman Archbishop of York: Thomas of Bayeu.

First Methodist: John Nelson, of Birstall, friend and co-worker of John Wesley.

First meeting of Yorkshiremen in London: December 3, 1679, when Dr. John Tillotson (Archbishop of Canterbury) "preached a sermon at the first general meeting of the gentlemen and others in and near London, born within the county of York."

First Yorkshireman to Australia: Captain James Cook, 1770.

First missionary to Australia: Samuel Marsden of Farsley, near Bradford. He preached the first sermon heard there on Christmas Day, 1814.

First Yorkshire Lord Mayor of London: Sir William Craven, born at Burnsall, in Upper Wharfedale.

First Yorkshire Chancellor of the Exchequer: Philip Snowden, of Cowling, near Keighley.

First bird photographer: Cherry Kearton, born at Thwaite, in Swaledale. His first camera was a box variety bought for 14 shillings in 1892. He used it to photograph a thrush's nest. Kearton published the first photographically illustrated bird book in the world. In 1903 he took the first motion pictures of a wild bird.

First Yorkshire president of the National Farmers' Union: James Turner later Sir James Turner, later Lord Netherthorpe, first elected to the office in 1945 at the age of 37. Retired 1959.

First Christian poet: Caedmon (Whitby Abbey, 7th century).

First discovery of "rock" music: Neddy Dick from Keld, the highest village in Swaledale, noticed the noise stones made as they clinked together when his walking disturbed them. He eventually managed to amass stones with a complete range of notes!

Pioneer for anti-slavery: William Wilberforce (1759-1833), who became Tory MP for Hull in 1780 and MP for Yorkshire in 1784.

First discovery of stainless steel: By Sheffield steelmaker Henry Brearley in 1913.

First mechanical woolcombing: Invented by Samuel Cunliffe Lister, first Baron Masham (1815-1906). He took out 150 patents for various inventions and also bought silk waste and converted it into velvet and carpets.

Invention of a shearing machine: By Enoch and James Taylor, thereby causing a great deal of industrial unrest.

Introduction of crayfish to Wensleydale: Supposedly by Walter Raleigh.

Designer and builder of the first steam locomotive (in the world): Matthew Murray, who arrived in Leeds jobless and penniless in 1790.

Women

First woman Catholic to suffer death in the reign of Elizabeth I: Margery Clythero, of York.

First "parachute" descent: In 1776 a young woman of Rigton, upset by an ill-starred love affair, went to Almscliffe Crag and flung herself over. Her skirts billowed out, and she landed safely!

First female incorporated accountant: Miss H. Mabel Claridge, of Bradford, who died in 1967, aged 81 years.

First straw hat wearer: Isobel Denton, of Beeston, Leeds, in reign of Charles I.

First maker of Sally Lunns: This delicacy was named after its inventor, Sarah Lunn, of Rothwell, near Leeds.

First woman to conduct a marriage ceremony in the Church of England: Deacon Sylvia Mutch pronounced Mr. Alistair Dearnley and Miss Heather Irvine man and wife in the church of St. Philip and St. James, York, at 12.15 p.m. on Wednesday, March 18th, 1987.

Last wife sold in Yorkshire: Details of wife-selling revealed at Leeds Police Court in January, 1926, when a husband parted with his spouse for £10. At Selby, in December 1862, a man parted with his wife for a pint of beer.

Claims to Fame

Man with the longest nose: Old Boots of Ripon. Could hold a piece of money between his nose and chin. His accomplishment was noted by a magazine in 1793.

Longest spell in bed: William Sharp, who lived at a farm called "The World's" at Laycock, near Keighley. He fell in love with a barmaid at the Devonshire Hotel, Keighley. She let him down on the day they were to have been married. William (then aged 30) returned home, went to bed and died in bed 49 years later following an attack of cramp.

Longest spell out of bed: For 40 years, Christopher Pivett, who died at York in 1796 at the age of 93. His house was accidentally burnt down. He resolved never to sleep in a bed again.

Longest sojourn underground: Geoff Workman, 88 days in Stump Cross Caverns, 1965.

Oldest man: Henry Jenkins, 169 years. He lived at Bolton-in-Swale (1500-1670). Henry claimed his long life was a consequence of "the virtues of cold water and raw onions and wearing flannel next to the skin from infancy." He remembered the Battle of Flodden Field because at the age of 10 or 12 he was sent to Northallerton with a cartload of arrows.

Oldest swimmer: Henry Jenkins swam the River Swale when he was over a hundred.

Oldest bride: Mrs. Winifred Clark was married in 1971 at Cantley, South Yorkshire, the day before her 100th birthday. The groom was 80.

Longest serving employee: Mr. Theodore C. Taylor served for 86 years with J.T. & T. Taylor of Batley, West Yorkshire, including 56 years as chairman.

Most descendants: The gravestone of Mrs. Sarah Crawshaw at Stones Church, Ripponden, Halifax, records that she died on Christmas Day, 1844, leaving 397 descendants.

Tallest man: Harry Cooper, known as "Alexander" lived and worked at South Skelton as an iron ore miner (mid 19th century). He grew 13 inches in five months when confined to bed, and at 23 was 8 feet 7¾ inches tall and weighed 406 lbs. He accompanied the monster elephant Jumbo to America and was exhibited in Barnum's Colossal Show.

Tallest twins: Jonathan and Mark Carratt of Maltby, South Yorkshire – the tallest twins in Britain at 6ft. 8in. and 6ft. 9in. respectively. They were born on 11th June, 1955.

Fattest man: Rev. Joseph Coltman of Beverley. He weighed 43 stones and had to be propelled along a special ramp to the pulpit by two men.

Meanest man: Old John Mealy Face, of Topcliffe, who was born in 1784. To safeguard his flour when going out he would press his face into the flour at the top of the bin, and then put his face back into the impression on returning.

Greatest walker: Possibly a Horsforth man, Foster Powell, who was born in 1734. He walked from London to York and back in five and a half days in 1773. The time included stops. Powell also walked 100 miles in 23½ hours.

Bell-ringer who rang the most peals: J. Bradley, senior bell-ringer at Bradford Cathedral in 1930s (about 400 peals).

Most famous signature: Robert Thompson of Kilburn, a woodcarver, used a mouse as his signature. He was so well known that a letter addressed only to "The Mouseman, England" reached its destination.

Greatest knit: Mrs. Gwen Matthewman of Featherstone, West Yorkshire, could handknit at a speed of 111 stitches per minute according to a test at Phildar's Wool Shop in Central Street, Leeds in 1980. We have it on good authority that her fingers never left her hand!

Most persistent driver: Mrs. Miriam Hargrave of Wakefield finally passed her driving test in 1970 at the age of sixty-two – her fortieth attempt.

Most unsuccessful Parliamentary candidate: F.R. Lees (Temperance) Ripon is believed to have been the only candidate in Britain ever to have received a nil vote. He notched up this dubious honour in 1860.

Only prophetess to give her name to an insect: Mother Shipton, the famous prophetess who lived in a cave beside Dropping Well, Knaresborough, had a moth named after her.

Most eccentric personality: Jimmy Hirst, buried at Rawcliffe, must rank as the favourite contender. He was recognisable by his yellow boots, rainbow waistcoat and a hat which sported a nine-foot brim. He tried to design wings so that he could fly. He failed. Another of his ploys was a carriage shaped like a Chinese hat.

Most optimistic playwright: Tate Wilkinson, the 18th Century manager of York Theatre Royal, rewrote *"Hamlet"* with a happy ending.

Most "polished" performance: In February 1982, four teenagers from the Sheffield Citadel Band of the Salvation Army showed a clean pair of heels – well, 6,780 pairs to be precise, when the cleaned 6,780 pairs of shoes (with the feet still inside them!) in eight hours.

Longest kiss of life: In August, 1981, five members of the St. John Ambulance Clifton Division, York, performed the kiss of life on a dummy for 240 hours with 224,029 inflations.

Sweetest lass of Richmond: Frances I'Anson of Hill House. She married Leonard McNally in 1787 and he wrote the song about her *Sweet Lass of Richmond Hill.*

Only Town Crier to have cried from three Mansion Houses in one day: Ted Corney of Doncaster at Doncaster, York and London on August 28th, 1985, sponsored by Doncaster Hospital Radio.

GRAVE CONCERNS

Giggleswick: The tomb of a 15th century knight was found, during church restoration work, to contain his horse, too.

Bradford, near Sheffield: There is still an ancient watch house, near the churchyard gate. It was built in 1745 to guard the graves from bodysnatchers.

Newburgh Priory: Said to contain the headless body of Cromwell in a sealed tomb.

York: Dick Turpin's tombstone (a modern replacement of the original) can be seen in St. George's churchyard. He was hanged at the York Tyburn on the Knavesmire in 1739.

Bingley: In the churchyard is the grave of Hezekiah Briggs – a sexton who interred over 7,000 corpses.

Haxby: The site of the gravestone of "Rash Tom" Holtby who drove the last stagecoach from Edinburgh to York.

Rossington: Charles Bosville, king of the gipsies, was buried here. After his death in 1708 it was the custom of the gipsies to visit his grave once a year and pour a flagon of ale over it.

Oakworth: Here lies the "Old Gentleman's Grave". When James Mitchell died over a hundred years ago, he ordered a servant to roll a big stone down the hill from his home at Oldfield Hall. Wherever the stone came to rest he should be buried.

Flamborough: St. Oswald's Church contains the tomb of Sir Marmaduke Constable, a commander at the battle of Flodden field. However, he didn't meet his demise on the battlefield – he died in 1528 after supposedly drinking water and swallowing a toad, which ate his heart away.

Slingsby: At the church is Wyville's tomb. It is said that he "with his dog did kill a monstrous serpent that lived and preyed on passengers on the road to Malton."

Kirklees Hall: The grounds reputedly contain the grave of Robin Hood, said to have shot his last arrow from the nearby Priory.

Fighting Talk

Most casualties lost in battle on British soil: Between 28,000 and 38,000 when 36,000 Yorkists defeated 40,000 Lancastrians at the Battle of Towton, near Tadcaster, on 29th March, 1461.

Chief Yorkshire land battles: Winwidfield 655, Dore 829 ("King Egbert of Wessex led his army to Dore in the Year AD829 against King Eanred of Northumbria by whose submission King Egbert became First Overlord of All England", Stamford Bridge 1066, the Standard 1138, Myton Meadows 1319, Boroughbridge 1321, Byland Abbey 1322, Bramham Moor 1408, Sandal 1460, Towton 1461, Tadcaster 1642, Leeds 1643, Wakefield 1643, Adwalton Moor 1643, Hull 1643, Selby 1644, Marston Moor 1644.

Site of a battle fought to settle the fishing rights in a Yorkshire lake: On the banks of Hornsea Mere in 1260 between the monks of St. Mary's, York and Meaux. York were victorious.

First enemy aircraft to be brought down in England during World War II: Crashed two miles west of Whitby on 3rd February, 1940.

Arncliffe Church in Littondale has two records of soldiers who went to war – one is a list of those who went to World War One, the other lists the soldiers who went to Flodden Field in 1513.

Dogged by Disaster

In Yorkshire and other northern counties there is a belief in a ghost dog called The Padfoot, about the size of a small donkey, black with shaggy hair and with large eyes like saucers. It follows people about or waylays them in lonely spots, and is regarded as a precursor of death. People say that they have heard it following them, and making a strange padding sound with its paws.

TALES OF THE UNEXPECTED

Oldest ghosts still reported: Sightings are still claimed of Roman soldiers marching through the cellars of the Treasurer's House, York Minster, after 1,900 years. When the caretaker spied them, he couldn't understand why he could only see them from the knees upwards until he was told the original Roman road was that corresponding distance further below!

Fairies have been photographed at Cottingley, near Bingley! Sir Arthur Conan Doyle believed the pictures to be true but in recent years they have been proved to be a hoax.

The hump-back bridge at Gunnerside in Swaledale is said to be haunted by a headless dog. There may be a tenuous connection between this and the fact that a nearby hamlet rejoices in the name of Crackpot!

At a cave called Navvy Noddle Hole at Elbolton Hill, above Thorpe, the bones were found of twelve men sitting in a ring, 20 centuries after they had died.

At Helmsley, the 16th Century Canon's Garth is said to be haunted by a beautiful nun who walks at midnight.

At Nunnington, on a dark night near Cauklass Bank, the sounds of a coach and horses have been heard.

King Arthur and the Knights of the Round Table are said to be laid to rest in a secret chamber beneath Richmond Castle but they will rise again if the nation is in peril!

A petrifying well at Mother Shipton's Cave at Knaresborough turns everyday objects into stone.

How t'First Yorkshire Pudding were Made

Eh waiter, excuse me a minute
I'm not finding fault – but dear me
Taties is lovely and beef is alreit
But what sort o'pudding can this be?

It's what – Yorkshire Puddin? Now
    cum, cum, cum, cum,
It's what – Yorkshire Puddin yer say?
I'll grant yer it's some sort o'puddin,
    owd lad
But not Yorkshire puddin, nay, nay.

Now reit Yorkshire Puddin's a poem in
    a batter,
T' mek it's an art, not a trade
So just listen t'me and I'll tell t'thee
How t'first Yorkshire Puddin were made.

A young angel we t'day off from 'eaven
Were flying abaht o'er Ilkley Moor
When t'angel, poor thing, got cramp
    in a wing
An'come down at an owd woman's door.

T'owd woman said "Eee – it's an angel
By heck, I'm fair capped to see thee,
I've noan seen one afore, but thas
    welcome
Come in an' I'll mash thi some tea."

T'angel said "By gum, thank you kindly."
Though she only supped one mug o'tea,
Ate two drippin slices and one
    Sally Lunn,
Angels eat very lightly yer see.

Then t'owd woman looked at clock sayin'
"Ey up, t'owd fellers due 'ome soon from
    t'mill
You gerron wi yer tea, but please
    excuse me
I'd best go an mek puddin fer Bill."

Then t'angel jumped up and said
"Gie us it 'ere, flour, water, eggs, salt
    and all
An I'll show thee how we meks puddins
Up in 'eaven for Saints Peter and Paul."

So t'angel took bowl and stuck a wing in
Stirring i round, whispering "Hush"
An' she tenderly ticked t'mixture
Like an artist ed paint wi a brush.

Then t'owd woman asked: "Ere, wor is it
T'secret of puddins made up above?"
"It's nowt i'flour or water," said t'angel
"Just mek sure that yer mek it wi love."

When it wer done, she popped it in
    t'oven
"Give it nobbut ten minutes" she said
Then off t'angel flew, leavin' first
    Yorkshire Puddin
That ivver were properly med.

An' that's why it melts in yer gob just
    like snow
An' as light as a maden's first kiss
As soft as the fluff on t'breast of a puff
Not elephant's leather like this!

FOOD FOR THOUGHT

Largest "chip hoil" (in the world): Harry Ramsden's famous fish restaurant at White Cross, Guiseley was established in 1928. The restaurant today serves over one million customers a year who munch their way through a staggering 240,000lbs of haddock and 544,000lbs of potatoes.

In October 1988 during its Diamond Jubilee celebrations Harry's broke its own World record by serving 10,182 customers in one day when it served fish and chips at 1928 prices – 2p!

Biggest ever feast: At Cawood, near Selby in 1464. The mammoth spread was hosted by a newly appointed Archbishop of York, George Neville, and the menu included 1,000 sheep; 2,000 pigs; 500 deer; 15,000 birds and 4,000 tarts!

First turkey: Introduced to England by the Strickland family of Boynton near Bridlington.

Largest pie: The villagers in Denby Dale are renowned for their pioneering pie-making. Their first enormous pie was made in 1788 to celebrate King George III's return to sanity. Another of their pies caused their plans to come unstuck when it stuck in the oven – and the pie of 1887 was so "high" it had to be given a decent burial. The six-ton pie of 1964 financed the purchased of the village hall. The dish alone weighed a ton and a half and was 18 feet long, 6 feet wide and 18 inches deep. And the ingredients? Ten bullocks, a ton and a half of potatoes, half a ton of flour, five cwts of lard and fifty gallons of gravy . . .

Largest consumption of oysters: Mr. Jaconelli, the world oyster-eating champion, hails from Scarborough.

Most famous cheese: Wensleydale, made from sheep's milk, introduced to the area by Cistercian monks of Jervaulx Abbey.

Firm with the most "relish": Yorkshire Relish has been made by Goodhall & Blackhouse Ltd., Leeds, since 1837.

Most enterprising toffee makers!: The Mackintosh family of Halifax started business by offering free samples of their home-made toffee.

First Feast of Stamford Bridge: 1066 and all that heralded the first of the traditional Feasts of Stamford Bridge to celebrate King Harold's defeat over the invading Norwegians. The tradition ceased about 1870. On feast day, every householder was entitled to brew his own ale and sell it from his own doorstep. "Spear-pies" were the traditional feast day fare – these pies were shaped like a boat and filled with pear, in honour of a Saxon warrior who sailed beneath the old bridge at Stamford at the height of the battle.

Most disgusting meal: Probably a cure for whooping cough – an old Bilsdale remedy which recommended tucking into a bowl of broth made from the carcasses of nine frogs.

Fowl Play

A February issue of The Dalesman in 1955 mentioned a farmhand who could kill and pluck a chicken in twelve minutes. He wondered if he held the record for this feat, but a reader quickly countered his claim by recalling that a fish and poultry shop in Leeds in the thirties regarded a time of five minutes to be the hallmark of a good poultry man, although the reader had seen it done in a minute less.

The same reader saw a colleague skin and clean a rabbit in exactly 37 seconds. He also pointed out that a competition would be held at the forthcoming Otley Show for killing and plucking poultry. The identity of the victorious chicken plucker unfortunately remains a mystery. Although we tried to trace him, the bird had flown!

MORE "BIG" NEWS

Largest rocking stone: At Brandreth Crags near Blubberhouses. It is said to weigh 24 tons.

Largest sundial: 12 feet in diameter at Sundial Cottage, Seaton Ross.

Largest Bronze Age monolith (in Britain): In the churchyard at Rudston near Scarborough – a gritstone pillar 26 feet 6 inches tall.

Largest Neolithic "barrow": At Duggleby Howe near Wharram-le-Street. A large round barrow over 20 feet high – the largest of its kind in Britain, where a mass New Stone Age cremation supposedly took place.

Largest prehistoric monuments: The Devil's Arrows, a group of three gritstone monoliths in a field near Boroughbridge, a former coaching point on the Great North Road. Each is about 20 feet high and buried to a depth of five feet.

Largest football: seven feet, nine inches in diameter and 80lb in weight, made by Mitre Sports, Huddersfield.

The said it of Yorkshire

It is absolutely impossible for any of us, no matter how fond we may be of our native county, to comprehend its vast size. Folks who live outside the borders cannot form any conception of its enormous area, of the difference between its three Ridings, of the alterations in scenery, of the gulf which separates the men of its towns and cities from the men of the lovely dales and woodlands.

J.S. Fletcher

★ ★ ★

It is a land of pure air, rocky streams and hidden waterfalls. In the winter the roads are often impassable when the heavy snow falls and the high fells are a white wilderness where a man could easily lose his way and die. But on summer days when the sun beats down on the lonely miles these uplands are a paradise, the air heavy with the sweetness of warm grass, the breeze carrying a thousand scents from the valley below. I like my fellow men but there are times when it is wonderful to be utterly alone in a wide landscape. There aren't many places in England where you can do this, but you can do it in my Yorkshire.

James Herriot

★ ★ ★

The Dales have never disappointed me. I still consider them the finest countryside in Britain, with their magnificent, clean and austere outlines of hill and moor, their charming villages and remote whitewashed farms, their astonishing variety of aspect and appeal, from the high gaunt rocks down to the twinkling rivers.

J.B. Priestley

SPORTS AND COMPETITION

Cricket

Yorkshire have been county cricket champions 31 times and have been joint champions on two other occasions. Five times they have won the championship three or more years in succession. Yorkshire records show that 3,130 matches have been played in first class cricket since the county club was formed in 1863 and of these 1,360 have been won and only 545 lost.

In one day matches, Yorkshire have been Gillette Cup winners twice (1965/69) Benson and Hedges Cup Winners in 1987 and John Player League winners once (1983).

First county cricket match: Yorkshire v Norfolk, 1833.

First Roses Game: At Hyde Park Ground, Sheffield, 1849.

First president for Yorkshire: T.R. Barker, elected in 1863, when the county club was formed.

First Yorkshire captain: Roger Iddison, of Bedale (a professional).

The oldest recorded clubs: Heworth, 1784; Hallam, 1796; Otley 1820.

Greatest number of centuries: 112 by H. Sutcliffe between 1919 and 1939.

Highest score in a county match: 341 by G.H. Hirst v Leicestershire, 1905.

Four centuries in one innings: Achieved in 1896 v Warwickshire. Scorers were Sir F.S. Jackson (117), E. Wainwright (126), Lord Hawke (166) and R. Peel (210 not out). Three centuries in one innings have occurred on 16 occasions.

Highest opening partnership: 555 by Percy Holmes (224 not out) and Herbert Sutcliffe (313). Yorkshire v Essex at Leyton in 1932.

Highest number of runs in a season: 2,883 by Herbert Sutcliffe in 1932.

Highest scoring batsman: H. Sutcliffe – 38,558 runs. Average 50.2 in 768 completed innings.

Greatest wicket taker in first class cricket: W. Rhodes, 4,187 wickets at an average of 16.71.

Best Bowling: H. Verity, 10 wickets for 10 runs v Nottinghamshire at Leeds, 1932.

Highest number of wickets in a season: 240, taken by W. Rhodes in 1900.

Highest score in a county championship match: 887 v Warwickshire, at Birmingham, 1896.

Lowest score in a completed innings: 23 v Hampshire at Middlesbrough in 1965.

Highest test score v Australia: 364 by Sir Leonard Hutton at The Oval, 1938. This was also the longest innings in test matches (13 hours 20 minutes).

Most test wickets in a day: 14 by H. Verity, v Australia in 1934.

Most runs by an English player in test matches: 8,114 by G. Boycott. He played in 108 test matches scoring a total of 22 centuries – both more than any other Yorkshireman.

Highest number of catches in a season: 96 by James Graham Binks in 1960.

Highest number of times a "double" has been scored (1,000 runs and 100 wickets in the same season): 16 times by Wilfred Rhodes between 1903 and 1926.

Greatest number of consecutive seasons in which a player has performed the "double": 11 by George Herbert Hirst.

Only player to score 2,000 runs and take 200 wickets in the same season: George Herbert Hirst in 1906 (2,385 runs, 208 wickets).

Greatest number of appearances in County Championship matches: 763 by Wilfred Rhodes between 1898 and 1930.

Oldest man to appear in a test match: Wilfred Rhodes when he played for England v West Indies at Kingston, Jamaica in 1930. He was 52 years 165 days.

Largest crowd (in England): 158,000 at Headingley, Leeds, for the test between England and Australia (22nd-27th July, 1948).

Rugby League

Oldest clubs: Several were formed in 1895.

Highest individual score: George Henry "Tich" West (1882-1927) of Hull Kingston Rovers scored 53 points (10 goals and a record 11 tries) in a First Round Challenge Cup-tie v Brookland Rovers on 4th March 1905.

Record number of points in a season: 496 (194 goals, 36 tries) by Benjamin Lewis Jones (Leeds) in 1956-57.

Most tries in a match: 11 by George West (Hull Kingston Rovers) v Brookland Rovers in the Challenge Cup on 4th March 1905.

Most tries in a season: 80 by Albert Rosenfield in 1913-14. (All for Huddersfield).

Most points in a career: A total of 6,220 by Neil Fox between 1956 and 1979. (All points scored with Yorkshire clubs, notably 19 seasons with Wakefield Trinity).

Highest score: Huddersfield 119 v Swinton Park 2 (Rugby League Cup), 28th February 1914.

Longest unbeaten run: 40 cup and league matches by Huddersfield 1914-15 including 3 draws.

Most capped player: Mick Sullivan of Huddersfield, Wigan, St Helens and York played in 51 international games for England and Great Britain and scored a record 45 tries.

Player in most Challenge Cup Finals: Eric Batten (Leeds, Bradford Northern and Featherstone Rovers) played in eight including war-time guest appearances between 1941 and 1952. He was on four winning sides.

Youngest player: Harold Wagstaff (1891-1939) played his first league game for Huddersfield at 15 years 175 days; for Yorkshire at 17 years 141 days and for England at 17 years 228 days.

Largest crowd (at any Rugby League match): 102,569 when Warrington played Halifax in the Challenge Cup final replay on 5th May 1954 at Odsal Stadium, Bradford.

Hockey

Oldest club: Halifax, founded in early 1880s.

Number of clubs at present in Yorkshire County Hockey Association: 45.

Yorkshire player most capped for England: Norman Hughes, 105 (ex-England, ex-Great Britain captain).

Most capped player for Yorkshire: David Higham, 202.

Top club of the Eighties: Wakefield, League champions 1988, League Cup double 1988, hat trick of cup wins 1987, 1988, 1989.

Yorkshire's best season: 1984/85, winners of County Championship.

Squash

First meeting of Yorkshire Squash Rackets Association: September 2nd, 1936.

First League: 1961. Consisted of seven clubs – Halifax, Sheffield, Harrogate, Hull, Heaton, Huddersfield and Catterick.

First fees: In 1936, affiliation fees of 10 shillings per court provided the foundation for squash activities.

First League Competition: January 1961. Won in its inaugural year by Queens. A second division was added in 1969, a third in 1970 and a fourth in 1971.

Earliest junior tournaments: 1949/50.

Present competitive events: The County League now has more than 100 teams as well as a knock-out cup, the County Closed, an Inter County side, plus extensive junior events.

Most wins: Terence Pickering from Abbeydale holds the record of 14 titles in the County Closed, although more recently Ian Robinson has won eight consecutive titles.

Most times capped for England: Ian Robinson (55 times). Ashley Naylor (29 times between 1981-86).

Inter County Championships: Yorkshire has gained 12 victories in the last 14 seasons.

Veterans' Inter-County Championships: Won by Yorkshire in 1984, 1985 and 1986.

Longest-serving President: Mike Grundy served as president for 25 years, his term of office commencing in 1962.

Athletics

The following are Yorkshire County Amateur Athletics Association's Best Championship performances.

Track Events

400 Metres Hurdles (Junior): 54.7 seconds by I.C. Welch, Leeds City A.C., 1981.

400 Metres Hurdles (Senior): 51.2 seconds by S.J. Sole, Hallamshire H., 1984.

100 Metres (Junior): 10.8 seconds by D. Artley, 1972; A. Slack, 1978; I. Simpson, 1984.

100 Metres (Senior): 10.6 seconds by I.D. Green, Luton A.C. 1972/73.

800 Metres (Junior): 1 minute, 52.0 seconds by J. Ashton, Wakefield H., 1975.

800 Metres (Senior): 1 minute, 45.6 seconds by S.N. Coe, Hallamshire H., 1978.

400 Metres (Junior): 48.5 seconds by S. Houlton, 1978; P. Crampton, 1986.

400 Metres (Senior): 46.8 seconds by A. Slack, Wakefield H., 1986.

110 Metres Hurdles (Junior): 15.2 seconds by D. East, Army A. College, 1976.

110 Metres Hurdles (Senior): 14.7 seconds by M.A. Johnson and B. McStravick, 1984.

5,000 Metres (Senior): 13 minutes, 59.8 seconds by D.A. Slater and I.W. Gilmour, 1979.

1,500 Metres (Junior): 3 minutes, 50.7 seconds by A.D. Leach, Rotherham H., 1983.

1,500 Metres (Senior): 3 minutes, 39.1 seconds by S.N. Coe, Hallamshire H., 1982.

200 Metres (Junior): 22.1 seconds by I. Simpson, 1984 and L. Man, 1985.

200 Metres (Senior): 21.3 seconds by P. Cooke, City of Hull, 1980 and M. Wright, Leeds City, 1987.

3,000 Metres Walk: 12 minutes, 24.0 seconds by L. Morton, Sheffield Utd., 1985.

2,000 Metres Steeplechase (Junior): 5 minutes, 45.5 seconds by I.C. Howley, Longwood H., 1985.

3,000 Metres Steeplechase (Senior): 8 minutes, 58.5 seconds by D.M. Coates, Middlesbrough, 1974.

4 × 100 Metres Relay (Senior): 42.4 seconds by Leeds City A.C., 1984.

Field Events

Pole Vault (Junior): 4.83 metres by P. Phelps, Normanton F.H.S., 1986.

Pole Vault (Senior): 4.80 metres by P. Phelps, Normanton F.H.S. 1986.

Putting the Shot (Junior): 18.08 metres by J. Alderson, Middlesbrough, 1970.

Putting the Shot (Senior): 18.96 metres by A. Rowe, Doncaster P.W.A.C., 1962.

Throwing the Hammer (Junior): 61.82 metres by D. Smith, Hull Spartan A.C., 1981.

Throwing the Hammer (Senior): 61.00 metres by P. Gordon, Wolverhampton & B., 1984.

Triple Jump (Junior): 15.35 metres by M.R. Makin, Leeds City A.C.

Triple Jump (Senior): 16.22 metres by M.R. Makin, Leeds City A.C., 1981.

Throwing the Discus (Junior): 52.18 metres by S. Hall, Doncaster P.W.A.C., 1965.

Throwing the Discus (Senior): 56.52 metres by P. Gordon, Wolverhampton & B., 1986.

Long Jump (Junior): 7.34 metres by M.R. Makin, Leeds City A.C., 1981.

Long Jump (Senior): 7.50 metres by Derrick Brown, Longwood H., 1984.

High Jump (Junior): 2.00 metres by A. Oversby, Spenborough A.C., 1980.

High Jump (Senior): 2.06 metres by M. Butterfield, R.A.F., 1978.

Throwing the Javelin (Junior): 72.48 metres by M.C. Hill, Leeds City A.C., 1983.

Throwing the Javelin (Senior): 77.06 metres by M.C. Hill, Leeds City A.C., 1986 (old model).

Tug of War

A historic sport currently enjoying a revival. In England the sport was recognised by the Men's Amateur Athletics Association and was an Olympic sport until 1920. Many village sports in the Dales feature tug of war high on the programme of events.

Origins: Crompton Parkinsons of Doncaster had a works team which eventually sparked off a series of teams in the South Yorkshire area – Thorne YFC, Peglers Brass and Doncaster YFC, which joined to form the Doncaster & District T.O.W. Association in 1971.

Formation of Yorkshire County Association: Doncaster & District joined St. Austins T.O.W. club of Wakefield and Walkington T.O.W.

Country teams added to the Assocation: Long Rishton, Walkington and Skirlaugh from East Yorkshire; Huddersfield, Bradford and Leeds Irish from West Riding towns; the Yearsley Grove team from Huntington, near York; East Easington from Cleveland; Upper Wharfedale based at Grassington; and recently Selby YFC.

Most successful team: Thorne YFC (Thorne Young Farmers) now known as Thorne Farmers.

Longest holders of Pat Phoenix trophy (inaugurated 1962) for the Yorkshire Championships: St Austins T.O.W. club held this trophy for 12 years.

Oldest team: Probably St. Austins T.O.W. club founded in 1944 by six Irish miners. (At that time it was six aside). In 1955, they won the Northern Counties Athletic Association, the main competition in the North of England.

Bowling

Formation of County Bowling Association: 1932.

Number of clubs: 111.

Number of members: 4,148.

Number of times winners of the Inter County National competition (Middleton Cup): Six times, last being 1990.

Yachting

Oldest club: Royal Yorkshire, based at Bridlington, founded in 1847.

Newest club: Hull Marina, founded in 1983.

Highest water used: Fly Flats reservoir (1,320ft above sea level) by Halifax Sailing Club.

Lowest water: Used by Humbermouth Yacht Club at Humberstone.

Largest water: Grimwith Reservoir, the largest single sheet of water in Yorkshire.

Largest natural water: Hornsea Mere used by Hornsea Sailing Club.

Smallest water: Punden Reservoir at Haworth used by the West Yorkshire Fire Service Club.

Angling

Up-to-date information no longer appears to be kept on a county basis, but the following records were claimed up to 1977.

Largest trout: 10lb 11½oz., caught in the Ouse at Nun Monkton, August, 1963, by Eric Seddon. T. Lister, a Yorkshire farmer, claims to have caught a 14lb trout from the Wharfe. A trout of 17lb was reputedly taken in the Driffield area in 1832; it was 32 inches long with a girth of 21 inches.

Largest sea trout: 16lb 4oz., caught in Barmston Drain near Bridlington, 1964, by W. Burnham, of Beverley.

Largest grayling: 3lb 14oz., caught in Driffield canal in 1966 by D. Sawyer.

Largest barbel: 14lb 5oz., caught in River Ure, 1976 by B. Morland, Knaresborough.

Largest pike: 31lb, jointly held by W. Higgins of Knottingley, and R. Fox of Hull. Both fish (believed to be the same fish, in fact, as they were caught at the same mark and both were returned!) were landed from Hornsea Mere, East Yorkshire, 1964.

Largest dace: 1lb 4oz., by S. Chaffer, from the Ure (Wensleydale). (Equalled by Stephen Brennan, from the Wharfe at Wetherby, 1972).

Largest carp: believed to be 33lb 11oz. by D. Moulds from a private pond near York, 1965.

Largest chub: 7lb 15½oz. by P. Minton from Bushby Close on the Ouse, 1964.

Largest eel: 7lb from Hornsea Mere from the 1939/45 war. The angler's name is not known.

Largest gudgeon: 4oz. 3½drams by H. Smith of Leeds in the Wharfe at Boston Spa, 1965.

Largest roach: 3lbs 10oz. by W. Cutting, Hornsea Mere, East Yorkshire, 1917.

The opening of the trout season in Yorkshire is April Fool's Day.

Field Sports

Oldest hare-hunting pack: Penistone Harriers, dating to 1260.

Oldest grouse-shooting butts: Rushworth Moor, West Yorkshire, about 1830. The idea for butts originated from experience on Snailsden Moor.

Highest number of pheasants bagged in one shoot: 7,000 in two days, Warter Priory, near York, 1914.

Thomas, 6th Baron Walsingham, bagged 1,070 grouse (one gun) on 30th August, 1988.

Between 1867 and 1923, the 2nd Marquis of Ripon bagged 556,813 head of game.

Oldest hunt (in the country): Sinnington Hunt (headquarters at Kirkbymoorside).

Horse Racing

First introduced: By the Romans in 210 AD.

First racetrack: At Netherby, near Kirkby Overblow.

Oldest steeplechase: Kiplingcotes, founded 1619.

Oldest classic horse race: St. Leger, Doncaster, (run in the second week of September).

First St. Leger winner: South Yorkshire's Albaculia, on the 24th September, 1776.

Highest ever odds: 1,099,299 to 1 by a backer from Otley in 1975.

Heaviest weight carried: At a match in York in 1788, two horses each carried 30 stone.

Most Classics won by a trainer: 41 by John Scott of Malton between 1827 and 1863.

Mountaineering

First recorded climbs: At Almscliff in the 1870s.

Finest concentration of hard climbs: Malham Cove.

Biggest inland artificial overhang (in England): Kilnsey Crag (35 feet of roof). Climbed free in 1988.

Oldest regional club: Yorkshire Mountaineering club, formed in the Leeds/Bradford area.

Number of recognised routes: over 2,000 gritstone; over 1700 limestone. The numbers are ever increasing. (There are two climbing guides to the area – one covers gritstone, the other limestone areas).

Hang gliding

First introduced to Yorkshire: Around 1976. There are now about 150 members of the Dales Club.

Altitude record (British): 13,600ft. above sea level, set in July 1987 by Colin Rider from Pudsey, whilst flying above Mallerstang Common.

Cross Country Flights: There have now been several flights of over 100 miles starting from Wether Fell near Hawes. The best distance so far achieved is 136 miles to Skegness, by Peter Hargreaves from Bishop Auckland in September 1985. At the time it was the British Open Distance Record.

Octopush
Just in case you didn't know . . .

The game started about 30 years ago through sub-aqua clubs primarily to keep divers fit through the winter non-diving months. It's a hard, physical game played with two teams, six in each and four reserves. Goals are scored by pushing a puck along the bottom of a pool with a bat into a three metre long stainless steel gulley at each end of the pool.

First Yorkshire League: 1975 with just a few initial teams. Leeds, Halifax and Huddersfield (all active sub-aqua clubs).

Number of teams in Yorkshire: 16.

Main competitions: The Tetley Cup, for Yorkshire only. The Wilkinson Sword Trophy – a day's tournament between the best three teams in Yorkshire against the top three in the North West.

Top team in Yorkshire (1988-89): Leeds.

Motor Cycling

Number of clubs: Yorkshire is divided into two sections – 22 adult and youth clubs affiliated to the East Yorkshire Centre and 52 to the Yorkshire Centre which governs the western part of the county.

Number of members: 6,000 members promote over 500 events per year, nearly all of which are run off the road.

First Auto Cycle Union: Formed in 1907 as an organisation separate from the Royal Automobile Club, hence the "Auto".

Premier annual event: The Scott Trial, run at Arkengarthdale each October – the toughest sporting trial to be run anywhere in the world.

Wins: Yorkshire Centre celebrated its 25th win in Inter Centre Team Trials in 1991.

Ballooning

Number of hot air balloons in Yorkshire: About twenty.

Cost of an average balloon: £10,000 – £12,000.

British National Hot Air Balloon Champion: David Bareford of Kidderminster (1990).

Most important competitions: The 3rd World Hot Air Balloon Championships were held at Castle Howard in 1977 (90 competed). The British National Championships were held at the same venue in 1977. In 1984 the European Championships were held at York.

Other sports
Roller hockey

First father and son to be selected to represent Great Britain: Gerry and Paul Trott from Liversedge, West Yorkshire. (The first time in 50 years of the Roller Hockey World Championships). They were selected to play in Brazil in September, 1986.

Women's weightlifting

First ever native weightlifting championship: Held at Huddersfield Sports Centre in September 1986.

Youngest competitor: 14 years.

Oldest competitor: 41 years.

Lightest competitor: 6st 10lbs.

Heaviest competitor: 15sts.

Golf

Earliest records: Yorkshire Union of Golf Club records date back to 1894.

Number of courses: 157 in the Yorkshire/Humberside region.

Archery

Longest arrow shot: A. Webster of Sheffield, 847 yards, 0 feet, 3 inches.

Oldest archery club: Believed to be Ripon: it fell into decline and was revived in 1934. Competition for the "Antient Scorton Arrow", near Richmond, was instituted by Roger Ascham, a tutor to Queen Elizabeth I.

British record: York Round, possible number of points 1,296. At Meriden on 26 June 1983, Steven Hallard achieved 1,160 (Single Round).

Basketball

Highest score in the National Cup: 157 by Solent v Corby (57) in January 1990.

Longest Goal (British record): 75 feet, 9½ inches by David Tarbitt of Altofts Aces v Harrogate Demons. (Featherstone, January 1980).

Cyclo-Cross

Number of clubs: 43 affiliated clubs in the Yorkshire Cyclo-Cross Association.

First club: 1959.

Oldest annual event: Three Peaks Race (see "Three Peaks" section).

Cycling
First Cyclists' Touring Club: Harrogate 1878.

Road Cycling
Fastest man over 50 miles: At Boroughbridge, in June 1983, Ian Cammish in 1 hour, 39 minutes, 51 seconds.

Fastest woman over 50 miles: At Boroughbridge, July 1976, Beryl Burton in 1 hour, 51 minutes, 30 seconds.

Longest distance over 12 hours: At Wetherby, September 1967, Beryl Burton with a distance of 277.25 miles.

(All the above are British Competition records).

Windsurfing
First introduced to Yorkshire: 1978 (taken up by almost all existing dinghy clubs).

Biggest event ever held (in the North of England): Olley of Otley Speed Event, 9th/10th May, 1987.

Number of competitors in the above event: 70.

Fastest speed ever attained inland: 30.86 knots by Simon Basset (Halifax Sailing Club).

Cross Country
Formation of Yorkshire Cross Country Association: 1889 (covers Yorkshire and Derbyshire).

Present number of clubs: 95.

Winners of the Individual Title in the Yorkshire Cross Country Senior Title Championships: Four people have won this event five times each. Their records are as follows: E. Glover (Hallamshire Harriers) 1911, 1912, 1913, 1914, 1921. Ernest Harper (Hallamshire Harriers) 1924, 1925, 1926, 1930, 1931. Mike Baxter (Leeds City) 1970, 1971, 1975, 1977, 1978. Colin Moore (Bingley Harriers) 1983, 1985, 1987, 1989, 1991.

Yorkshire Dales Triathlon
First triathlon: Established 1984.

Length of swim: ¾ mile (Semerwater).

Length of cycling course: 42 miles through five dales – Wensleydale, Swaledale, Garsdale, Dentdale and Ribblesdale to Helwith Bridge.

Length of running course: 11 miles, including Penyghent summit. The toughest triathlon held in Britain, the cycling includes 4,000 feet of climbing and the running 1,500 feet of climbing.

Number of competitors: Average 150 annually. (August).

Fastest time: Steve Fenney of Reading in 3 hours, 48 minutes, 43 seconds.

Snooker
First maximum break scored in World Championships: At the Crucible Theatre, Sheffield, in 1983. 147 was scored by Cliff Thorburn (Canada) playing against Terry Griffiths.

World Amateur break record: At the TUC Club, Middlesbrough in 1978. 140 by Joe Johnson of Bradford.

Lacrosse
Highest scores (in the English Club Championship): Sheffield University with 30-5 v Hampstead in 1982 and 30-1 v Kenton in 1983.

Traditional Competitive Events
The oldest surviving sporting contest (in the world): The Antient Scorton Silver Arrow Contest dates back to 1673 when 22 archers competed on the village green. The contest became an annual event.

World coal-carrying contest: Held at Gawthorpe, near Ossett on Easter Monday. Competitors have to run nearly a mile, each carrying 50kg of coal. The current world record is 4 minutes, 6 seconds by David Jones of Melforth in 1991.

Knaresborough annual bed race: Established in 1966, a 2 mile 63 yard course crossing the River Nidd.

Fastest record: 12 minutes 16 seconds by runners from Harrogate Athletic Club (1989).

Yorkshire's Coat of Arms

A Flea, a Fly, a Magpie, 'an Bacon Flitch,
Is t'Yorkshireman's Coit of Arms.

And so it has been for many years, a gross libel on Yorkshire folk! The flea, it is said, represents shrewdness, the fly, hospitality. Magpies are linked with superstition, and a flitch of bacon is never any good until it is hung, like the Yorkshireman, it is said!

The following poem sums it up perfectly:

A Flea, a Fly, a Magpie, an' Bacon Flitch,
Is t'Yorkshireman's Coit of Arms,
An' t'reason they've chossen these things so rich
Is because they have all speshal charms.
A Flea will bit whoivver it can,
An' soa, my lads, will a Yorkshireman.
A Fly will sup wi' Dick, Tom, or Dan,
An' soa, by gow, 'ull a Yorkshireman.
A Magpie can talk for a terrible span,
An' so an' all can a Yorkshireman.
A Flitch is no gooid till it's hung, you'll agree,
No more is a Yorkshireman, don't you see?

Fell Racing

Fell facing has been widely recognised as an integral part of Yorkshire's rural heritage since deep into the last century, when dalesmen extending their upland passions for sport and hunting founded their own recreation inspired by impressive natural surroundings. These early events, raced up and down a neighbouring hillside, were often held informally as part of a local show, fair, festival or religious celebration.

Oldest literary record: In a 1922 edition of the "Craven Herald and Pioneer" newspaper was an article stating that the Lothersdale Sports, inclusive of fell race, were celebrating their 75th anniversary, but there are no records of 1847's first winner or precise course.

First Lothersdale fell race: Not necessarily 1847! It's often been muted that Olive Cromwell who named the village "Lo there's a dale" had raced his men up and down the fellside during camp training there, in readiness for the siege on Skipton Castle.

Most disputed fell racing record: For the Burnsall Fell Race, one of the first to record winners and winning times. The oft disputed record of 12 minutes, 59.08 seconds was accredited to Ernest Dalzell of Sheepfold, Keswick in 1910. It remained for 67 years until beaten by Fred Reeves of Coniston – undisputedly in 1977 with a time of 12 minutes, 42.02 seconds. Although the Fell race was traditionally held at Burnsall Feast Sports, neither of these records was attained at that event – both were established at special races. Dalzell's record was established in a special race held on September 10th, 1910 to settle controversy over the win by Tom Metcalfe of Hawes at the Feast Sports in 1908!

Most Burnsall victories: (Before the event became registered under Amateur Athletics' Association (AAA) laws in 1932, having previously been classed as "professional" or "open to all-comers"): By Jack James of Hincaster, Kirkby Lonsdale, 6 successive victories (1926-31 inclusive).

Most victories under the AAA regime: Peter Watson of Bramley and District Harriers (later to be known as Pudsey and Bramley AC) attained 7 victories between 1959 and 1969.

First Kilnsey Crag Race: 1899.

Record number of Kilnsey victories: By Bill Teasdale, M.B.E. of Caldbeck in the Lake District, 7 between 1949 and 1958. Teasdale also held the course record at one stage and on 22 consecutive occasions finished in the first 5. He might well have added further to that record but for the change in the traditional show date which saw him turn up a week late!

Current course record for Kilnsey: 7 minutes 35.8 seconds by Mick Hawkins of Grassington (1982). Hawkins also holds the Junior (under 17 record) of 8 minutes, 15.6 seconds (1978). He is one of only two people to have achieved the Junior-Senior winning double at Kilnsey. Norman Beck, Skipton was the first (1957 and 1963).

Most consecutive victories at any Yorkshire Fell Race: 11 by Fred Reeves at Embsay Fell Race between 1970 and 1980.

Only man to have won three Fell races in one day: Arthur ("Artie" or "Ant") Metcalfe who triumphed at Thoralby, Horton-in-Ribblesdale and Kirkby Malham during the 1920s.

The Three Peaks

(Ingleborough, Whernside and Penyghent)

First recorded traverse: Canon J.R. Wynne-Edwards and D.R. Smith in July, 1887, 10 hours.

Ski-crossing: C.R. Wingfield, 1909. He made a run from Nelson over the moors to Skipton and Grassington; over Gt. Whernside to Buckden; Buckden Pike to Aysgarth; from Hawes Junction over Wild Boar Fell to Kirkby Stephen; and thence over Nine Standards Rigg and The Calf to Sedbergh. Time taken was seven days.

First Ingleborough Mountain Race: May 22nd, 1934, won by Len Howarth in 1 hour 8 seconds. Distance to summit and back is 4½ miles. Formation of Three Peaks Club: 1944. Three Peaks of Yorkshire Club formed in 1967.

First motorised traverse: H.Q. Company of 12th Battalion the Parachute Regiment (T.A.) with Land Rover. Circuit completed in 11¾ hours.

First cycle traverse: December, 1958. Bradford Racing Cycling Club. They halted overnight at Ingleton. In October, 1959, cycle circuit completed by 14-year-old Kevin Watson in 6 hours 45 mins.

First foot-race: April 1954, organised by Preston Harriers and Athletic Club. Six competitors started, three finished. The start/finish was at the Hill Inn and the route was Ingleborough, Penyghent, Whernside. The winner was F. Bagley (Preston Harriers) in a time of 3 hours 48 minutes.

Foot-race record: race transferred to Horton-in-Ribblesdale in 1975): For the Chapel-le-Dale course, Jeff Norman (Altrincham) – 2 hours, 29 minutes, 53 seconds (April 1974). Jeff also holds the record number of wins (six times 1970-1975 inclusive). For the Horton-in-Ribblesdale course, J. Wilde (RAF Cosford) – 2 hours, 37 minutes, 30 seconds (1982). For the 1986 and subsequent races the course was altered again away from environmentally sensitive areas (Black Dub Moss, Stottering Ghyll etc.) which lengthened the course markedly. The record for this variation was set in 1991 by Ian Ferguson (Bingley Harriers) in 2 hours 51 minutes, 41 seconds.

First ladies race: 1979. Ladies race record: Sarah Rowell of Leeds City – 3 hours, 16 minutes, 29 seconds in 1991.

Record for men over 40: P. McWade, Clayton – 3 hours, 1 minute, 50 seconds (1989).

Record for men over 50: D. Ashton, Blackburn – 3 hours, 21 minutes, 42 seconds (1989).

Three Peaks of Yorkshire Club: Formed in 1967, it has around 40,000 members. To become eligible for invitation to join, walkers must achieve the three summit cairns and return to base (Penyghent Cafe, Horton-in-Ribblesdale) within the traditional time of twelve hours.

Only "clocking-in" machine for walkers world wide: Penyghent Cafe has a scheme whereby walkers complete cards designed to fit an ex-factory clocking-in machine.

First cyclo-cross: October 1st, 1961, organised by Bradford Racing Cycling Club.

Cyclo-cross record: distance altered from 25-35 miles in 1983. (Of these 35 miles, 16 miles is on the fells. The course is believed to be the toughest cyclo-cross in the world). Prior to 1983: Eric Stone (Otley) – 2 hours, 37 minutes, 33 seconds. (September 1971).

Since 1983: Tim Gould (Matlock) – 3 hours, 2 minutes, 48 seconds. (1988, his fifth win).

Most outstanding "marathon" performance: By Denis Beresford of Barnoldswick and Clayton-le-Moors Harriers. Completed the Three Peaks circuit three times in one day in 1979 in a time of 13 hours, 16 minutes.

Special Achievement: Until 1991, nine people had completed the race on at least 21 separate occasions and have been presented with a special award. John North of Rawtenstall and Clayton-le-Moors Harriers was fourth in the running race in 1978 and first in the cyclo-cross in 1981. By 1989, John Rawnsley, the organiser of the cyclo-cross, and Neil Orrell, had each competed in the event 28 times and John Rawnsley had walked or cycled the route more than 110 times.

Challenge Walks

A selection of walks that can be attempted at any time.

Lyke Wake Walk

40 miles across the North York Moors from Osmotherley to Ravenscar. (Ascent 5,000 feet).

First crossing: October 1st/2nd, 1955.

Fastest crossing: Mark Rigby, 4 hours, 41 minutes (1989).

Fastest crossing by a woman: Cath Proctor, 5 hours, 43 minutes (1991).

Fastest double crossing: (80 miles there and back), Arthur Puckrin in 1964, in 14 hours, 38 minutes. He also did a triple crossing on this occasion, 120 miles in 32 hours, 15 minutes, sleeping for five hours at Hamer on his third crossing. There have been many double crossings in two days, including two by women, Jane Saunders and Hilary Clarke.

Youngest Lyke Walker: 6 years, 11 months (Turton).

Oldest: Rev. A. Clarisford Morgan, 81, September, 1962.

Ski-crossings: (24 hours daylight allowed). W. Cowley, J. Cowley, C. Bosanquet, D. Rich – 17 hours ski-ing (plus 12 hours darkness spent in Goathland), March 2nd, 1963. There have been crossings on bicycles and attempts on horseback, but these are not recognised or encouraged by the Lyke Wake Club. Bogs on the route are highly dangerous to horses.

First man to complete 100 crossings: Louis Kulscar (1973).

First man to complete 200 crossings: The late Ben Hingston (1983).

Time Limit: 24 hours.

The Pennine Way

First of 14 designated long-distance footpaths in Britain. 270 miles long from Edale in Derbyshire to Kirk Yetholm in Scotland. (Ascent 27,000 feet).

Officially opened: 1965.

Fastest time: 3 days, 42 minutes by Brian Harney (Dark Peak Fell Runners and Rotherham Harriers), August 9th-12th, 1979.

The Dales Traverse

Start and finish: Kilnsey.

Distance: 25 miles.

Origins: In 1983 Wheatfields Hospice in Leeds did the inaugural walk which raised £18,500.

Number of recorded completions to date: 606.

Time limit: Badges and certificates available for those who complete in 12 hours.

The White Rose Walk

Newton-under-Roseberry – White Horse, Kilburn.

First devised: By the Yorkshire Wayfarers rambling club.

First completion: 1968.

Distance: Long route: 37 miles (Ascent 4,900 feet). Medium route: 34 miles (Ascent 4,800 feet). Short route: 31 miles (Ascent 4,000 feet).

Time limit: None.

The Rosedale Circuit

Start and finish: Rosedale Abbey.

First devised: By the Blackburn Welfare Society Rambling Section in 1973.

Distance: 37 miles (Ascent 4,000 feet).

Time limit: None.

The West Cleveland Circuit

Start and finish: Old Quarries car park, near Osmotherley.

First devised: By the rambling section of the Yorkshire Bank in 1976.

Distance: 26 miles (Ascent 4,100 feet).

Time limit: 12 hours (optional).

The Bilsdale Circuit

Start and finish: Newgate car park, Bilsdale.

First devised: By two Long Distance Walkers' Association members, Mike Teanby and Mike Smith in 1976.

First organised as a challenge walk: September 1979 by the North Yorkshire Group of the L.D.W.A. in order to promote the walk.

Distance: 28 miles (Ascent 4,000 feet).

Time limit: None.

The Samaritan Way

Start and finish: Guisborough.

First devised: In 1978 when it was officially opened by Lord Guisborough. So called because the proceeds from the sale of badges and certificates are forwarded to the Teesside Samaritans.

Distance: 38 miles (Ascent 4,500 feet).

Time limit: 24 hours (optional). The walk can be completed within 24 hours, or over a number of days or occasional weekends.

The Swale Watershed Walk

Start and finish: Richmond.

First devised: By members of the Swale Outdoor Centre in 1970 as a weekend expedition only to be attempted between November and March.

Distance: 59 miles (Ascent 5,650 feet).

Time limit: 48 hours.

Challenge Events

A selection of challenge walks held on a specific date.

The North York Moors Crosses Walk
Start and finish: Goathland.

First devised: In 1971 to raise funds for the Scarborough and District Search and Rescue teams.

First completion: July, 1972.

Distance: 54 miles (Ascent 4,000 feet).

Time limit: 24 hours.

Fellsman Hike
Ingleton – Threshfield.

First devised: In 1962 by the Keighley Scout Service Team. (The first challenge event in the North of England).

Distance: 60 miles (Ascent 11,100 feet).

Time limit: Restricted by checkpoint deadlines. Regarded as the most gruelling hike in the country.

The Six Dales Hike
Settle – Skipton-on-Swaledale.

First devised: In 1956 by the North-West Leeds Scout District.

Distance: 42 miles (Ascent 3,000 feet).
Actual event restricted to members of the Scout and Guide movement in Yorkshire although the route is entirely on rights of way.

Time limit: Restricted by checkpoint deadlines.

The Swaledale Marathon:

Start and finish: Reeth.

First devised: 1979 by the Swaledale Outdoor Club.

Distance: 23 miles (Ascent 3,000 feet).

Time limit: 10 hours.

The Ulkfil Stride

Start and finish: Buckden.

First devised: In 1979 by the West Yorkshire Group of the L.D.W.A.

Distance: (Dual distance) 33 miles (Ascent 15,000 feet)/ 24 miles (Ascent 3,500 feet).

Time limit: 11 hours.

Tailpiece – Back to the Future

The first Northern Convention of Contact (U.K.) – a flying saucer-watchers' association was held at Ilkley in 1967. Disappointingly no U.F.O.s put in an appearance. But it isn't surprising that U.F.O. enthusiasts have been active in Yorkshire. Since 1947 when a Barnsley policeman reported a greyish white disc travelling fairly swiftly across the sky, Yorkshire has had its fair share of Unidentified Flying Objects. Few have been sensational sightings and no one has claimed to see little green men: what is significant is the similarity of the reports which have usually come from ordinary people who have been highly surprised to peer out of their bedroom windows at night and see a reddish-blue object with a tail which broke up over an hour (Guiseley, 1964) or circle of lights like a fairground roundabout which passed over to the sound of muffled booms (Bradford, 1971).

One of the most unusual sightings was that of a Batley man in 1968 who claims to have almost driven beneath a flying saucer which hung over the road at night. "I stopped and got out for a closer look. There seemed to be a lot of red lights hanging over the road in a rough diamond shape. The others were what seemed to be a row of portholes."

Yorkshire Records
A comprehensive index